Large Print
Color By Numbers For Adults
Jumbo Coloring Book of Birds, Flowers, and More
Simple Anti Anxiety Coloring Relaxation

BY COLOR QUESTOPIA

Copyright © 2021

All rights reserved. No part of this publication may be reproduced, distributed, or transmitted in any form or by any means, including photocopying, recording, or other electronic or mechanical methods, without the prior written permission of the publisher

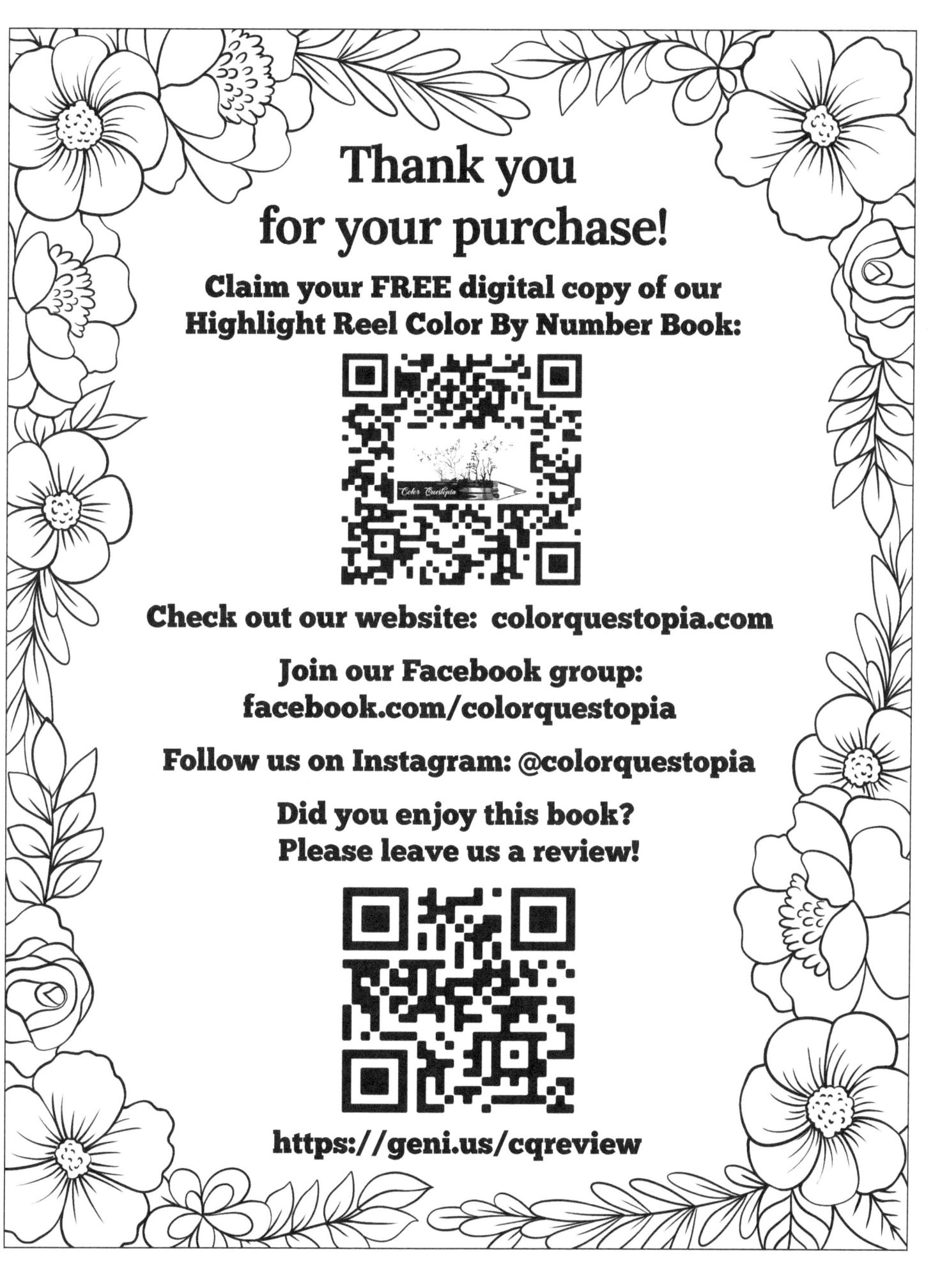

Color By Number Tips

1. **Relax and have fun**
   Let your cares slip away as you color the images. Take your time. Coloring is a meditative activity and there's no wrong way to do it. Feel free to color as you listen to music, watch TV, lounge in bed- do whatever relaxes you most! You can also color while you're out and about- on the train or at a cafe- take the book with you anywhere you go. Coloring is therapeutic and is great for stress relief and relaxation!

2. **Colors corresponding to each number are shown on the back cover of the book - THIS BOOK HAS OUR NEW COLORING SYSTEM WHERE EVERY COLOR IN EVERY BOOK IS SHOWN ON THE BACK OF THE BOOK**
   Each number corresponds to a color shown on the back of the book. Because this is our new system, there may be colors and numbers on the back that aren't in this book- that's totally okay. Just follow the numbers on the images in this book, and match those numbers to colors. You can match the color as closely as you like- but feel free to change the color or the shade if you don't have the exact color match- that's totally fine. Although this is a color by number book, it's completely okay to get creative and color the images with whichever colors you like and have. The numbers are there to be a guide and to allow you to color without having to focus your energy on choosing colors.

3. **Choose your coloring tools**
   Everyone has their favorite coloring markers, crayons, pencils, pens- even paints! Feel free to color with any tool that you like! If you choose markers or paints, we recommend putting a blank sheet of paper or cardboard behind each image, so that your colors don't run onto the next image.

5. Red
8. Light Yellow
9. Yellow
11. Bright Orange
12. Light Orange
14. Orange
18. Medium Brown
22. Light Green
24. Green
28. Light Pink
30. Pink
31. Hot Pink
34. Purple
37. Violet
39. Baby Blue

40. Sky Blue
41. Light Blue
42. Medium Blue

1. Black
5. Red
9. Yellow
11. Bright Orange
14. Orange
19. Brown
22. Light Green
23. Medium Green
24. Green
25. Army Green
26. Dark Green
28. Light Pink
29. Medium Pink
35. Light Violet
37. Violet

39. Baby Blue
40. Sky Blue
41. Light Blue
42. Medium Blue

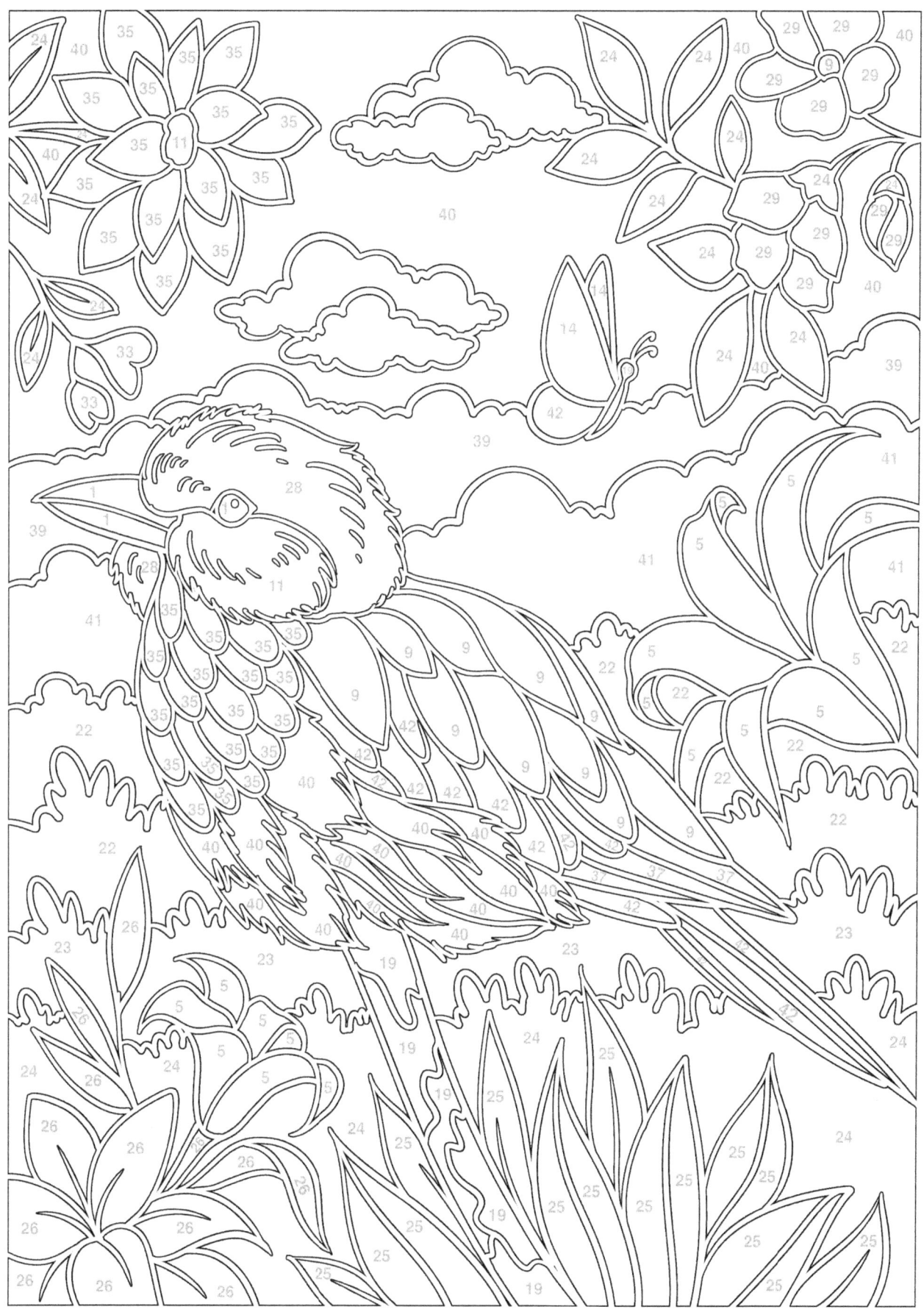

5. Red

9. Yellow

12. Light Orange

18. Medium Brown

22. Light Green

24. Green

28. Light Pink

30. Pink

31. Hot Pink

37. Violet

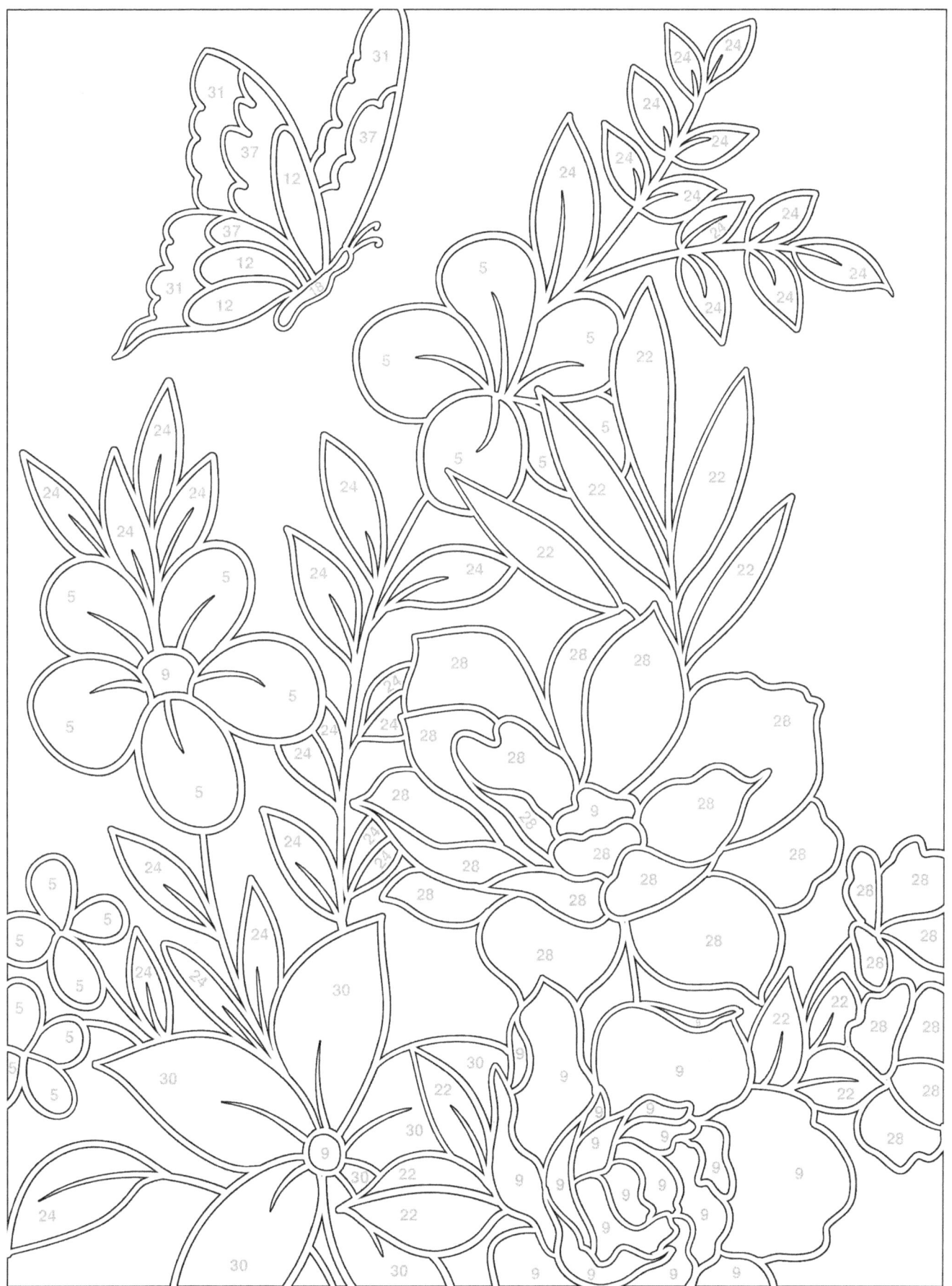

4. Medium Red

5. Red

7. Lemon Yellow

8. Light Yellow

9. Yellow

11. Bright Orange

14. Orange

17. Light Brown

18. Medium Brown

19. Brown

21. Neon Green

23. Medium Green

24. Green

26. Dark Green

30. Pink

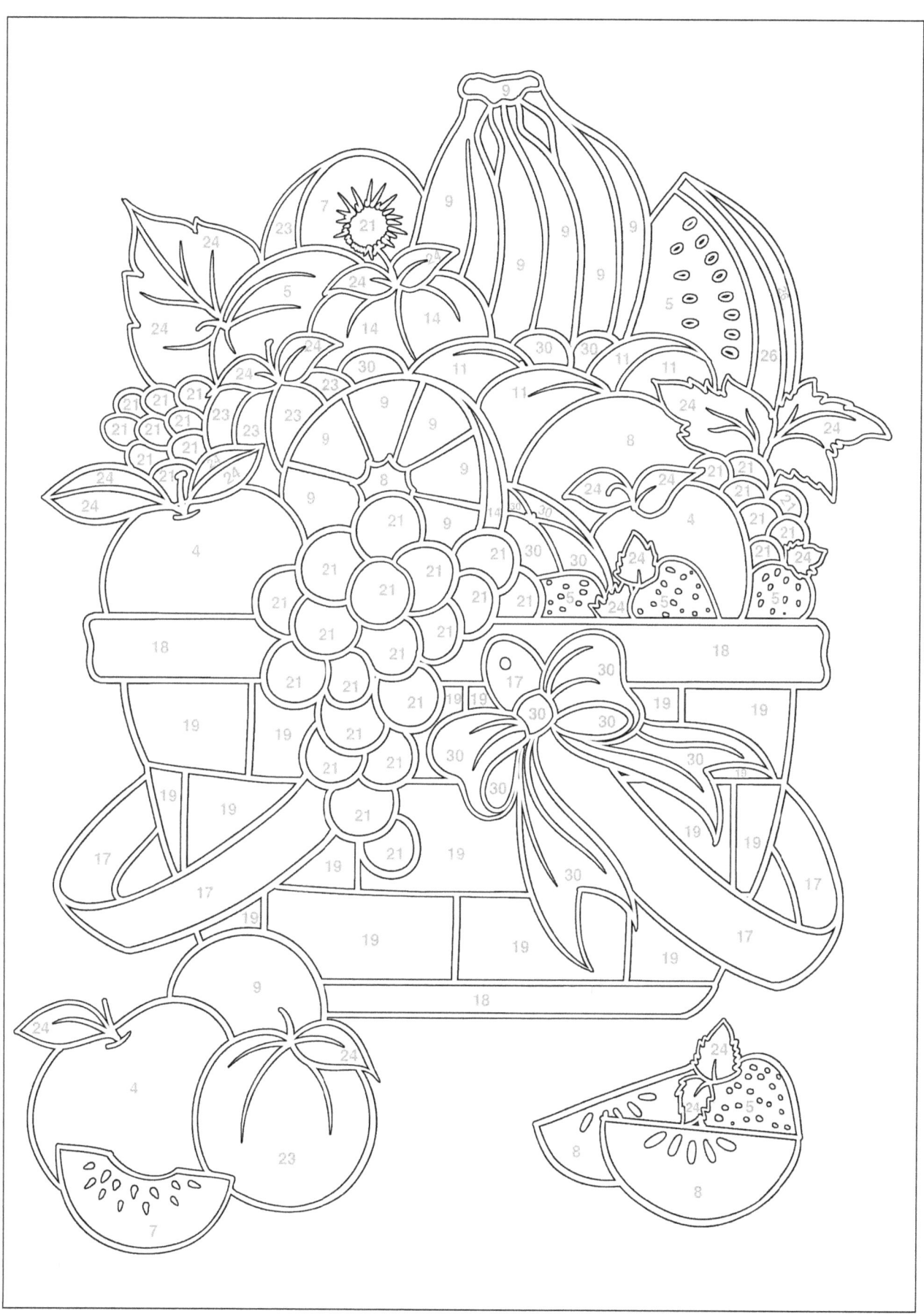

1. Black
5. Red
7. Lemon Yellow
9. Yellow
10. Dark Yellow
11. Bright Orange
12. Light Orange
13. Medium Orange
19. Brown
22. Light Green
23. Medium Green
24. Green
26. Dark Green
27. Peach
28. Light Pink

30. Pink
33. Medium Purple
39. Baby Blue
40. Sky Blue
42. Medium Blue

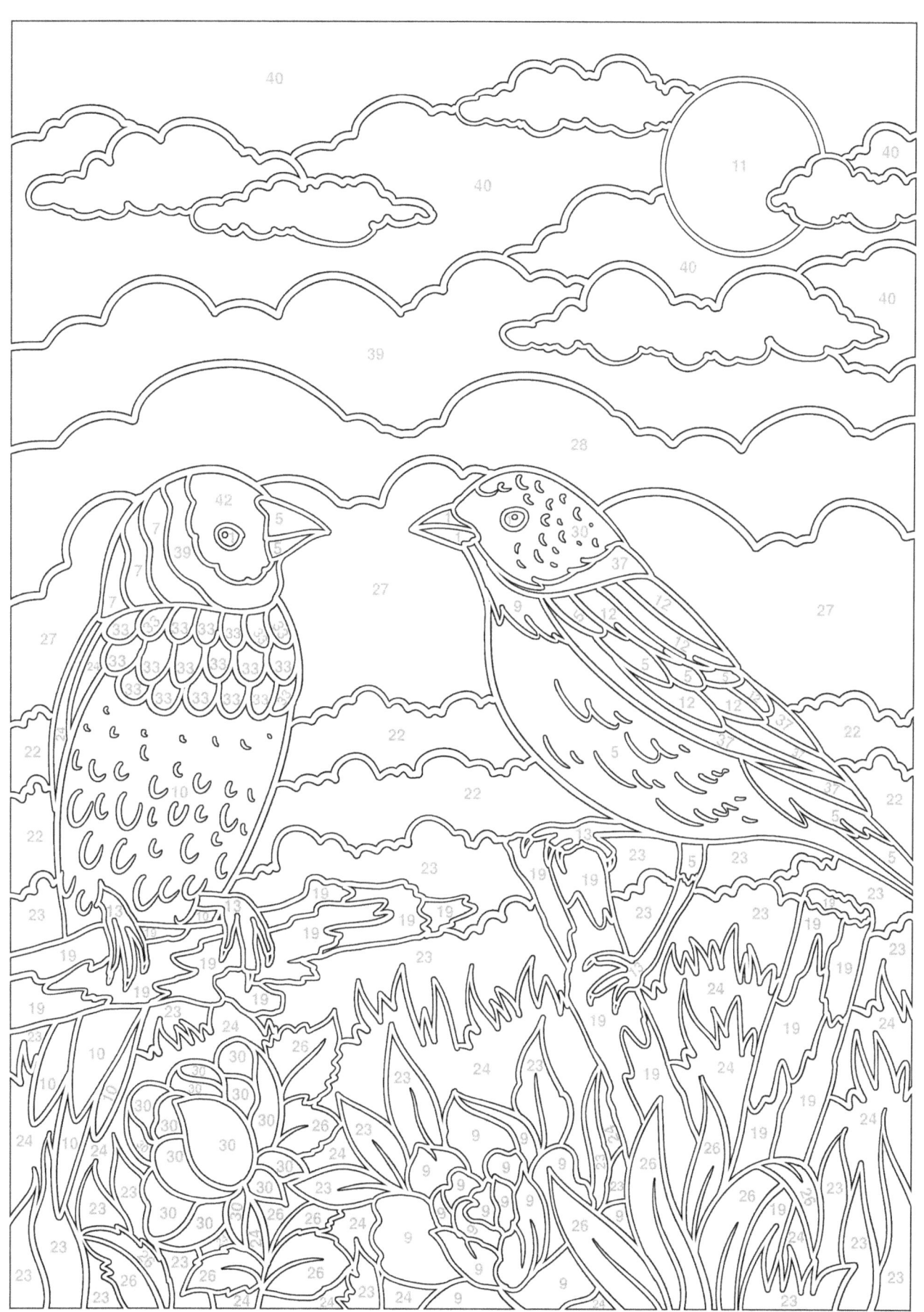

1. Black

5. Red

9. Yellow

12. Light Orange

14. Orange

23. Medium Green

28. Light Pink

30. Pink

33. Medium Purple

37. Violet

39. Baby Blue

41. Light Blue

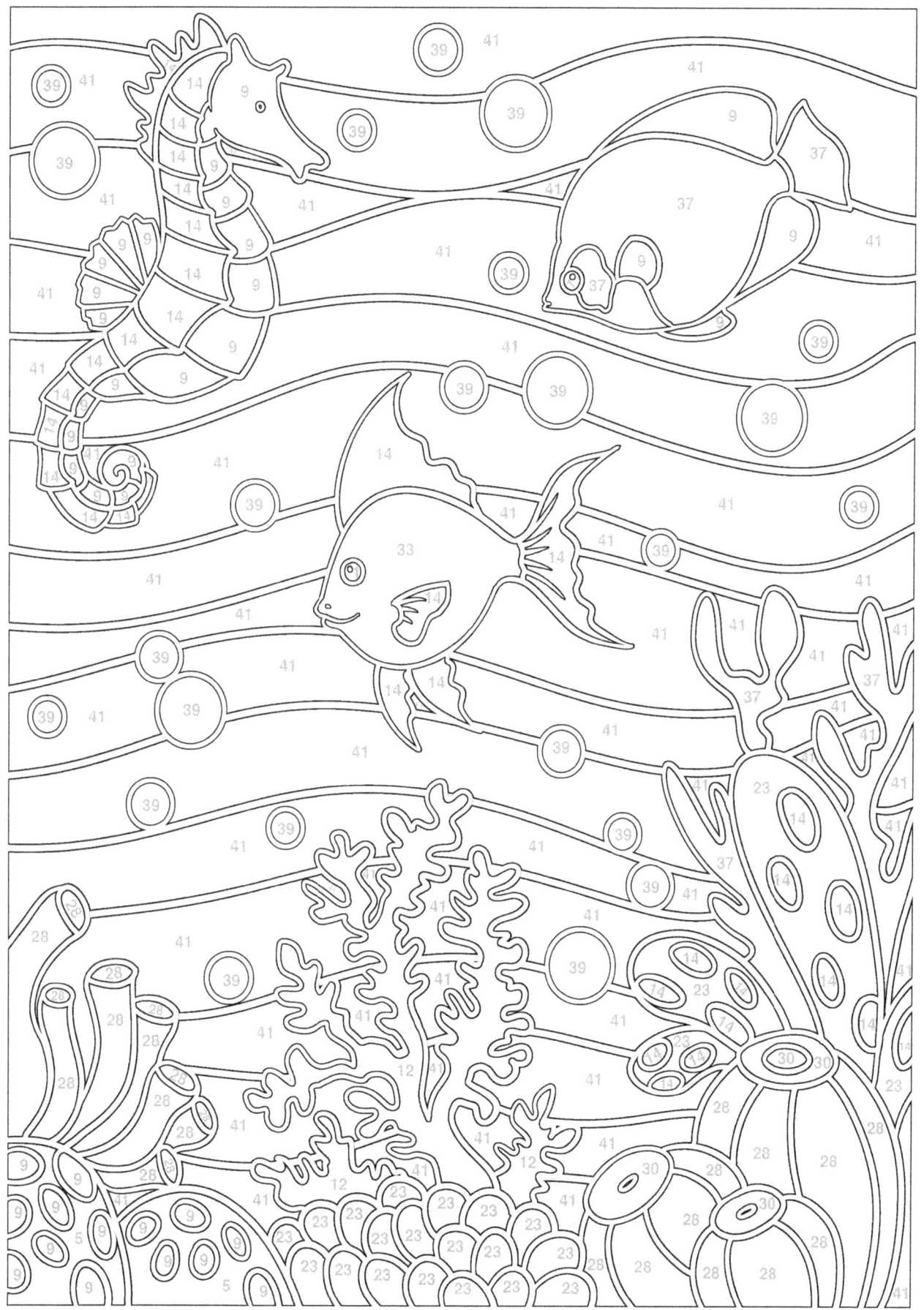

1. Black
5. Red
17. Light Brown
22. Light Green
23. Medium Green
24. Green
26. Dark Green
29. Medium Pink
30. Pink
40. Sky Blue
46. Beige

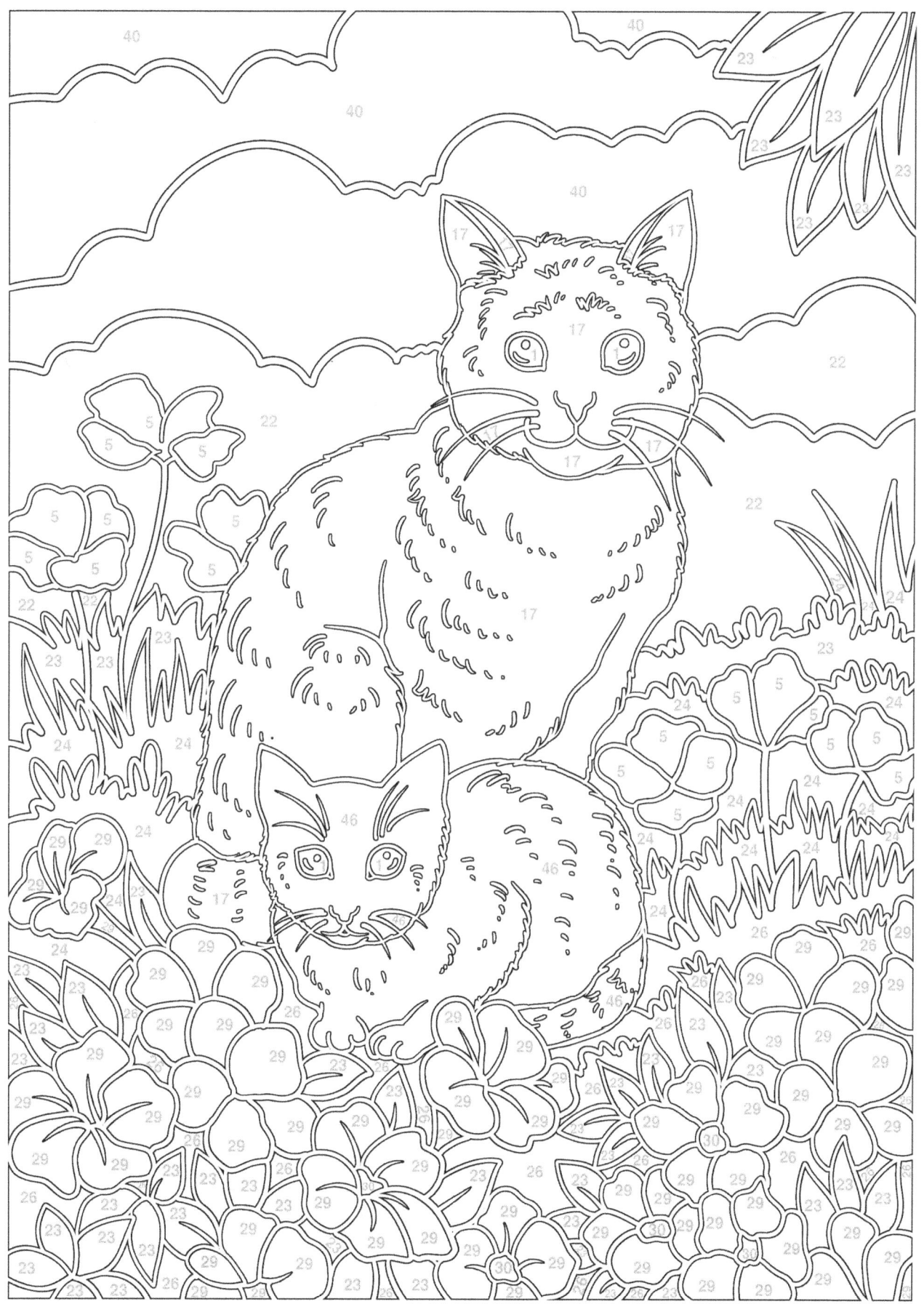

5. Red

9. Yellow

14. Orange

18. Medium Brown

23. Medium Green

24. Green

28. Light Pink

30. Pink

34. Purple

39. Baby Blue

40. Sky Blue

42. Medium Blue

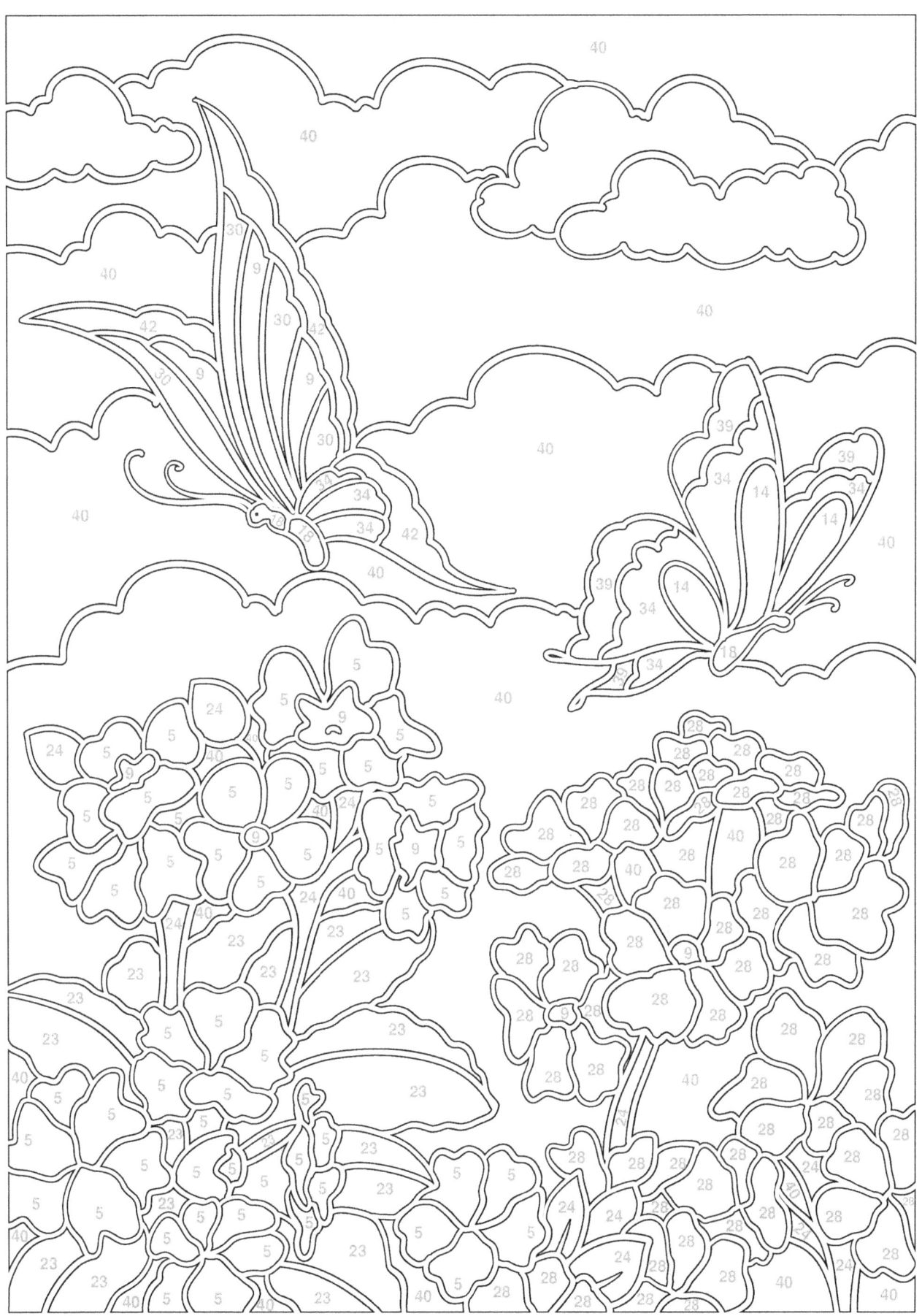

8. Light Yellow

9. Yellow

14. Orange

18. Medium Brown

22. Light Green

24. Green

26. Dark Green

29. Medium Pink

34. Purple

42. Medium Blue

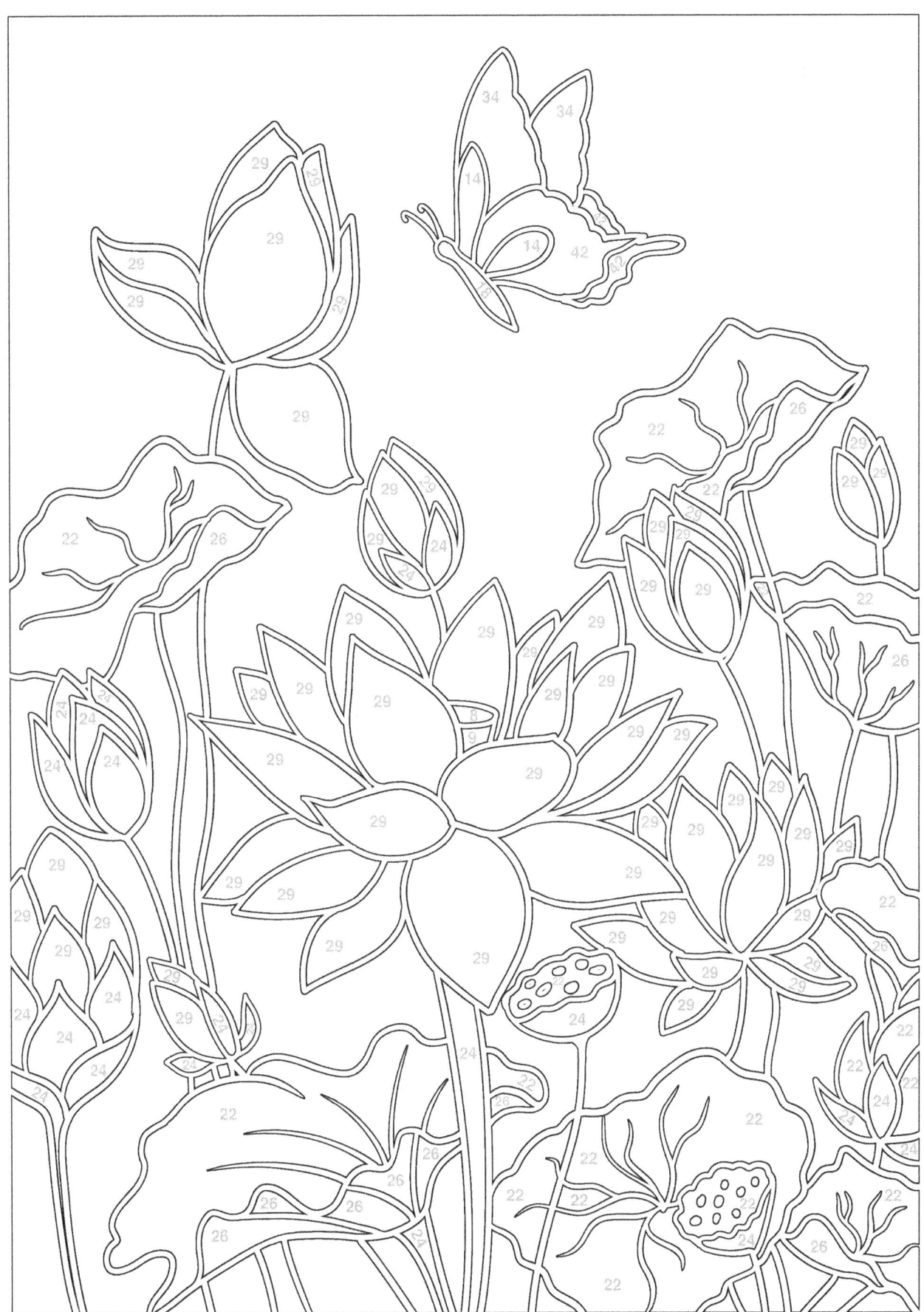

1. Black
8. Light Yellow
9. Yellow
13. Medium Orange
14. Orange
22. Light Green
23. Medium Green
24. Green
25. Army Green
27. Peach
30. Pink
35. Light Violet
39. Baby Blue
40. Sky Blue
41. Light Blue

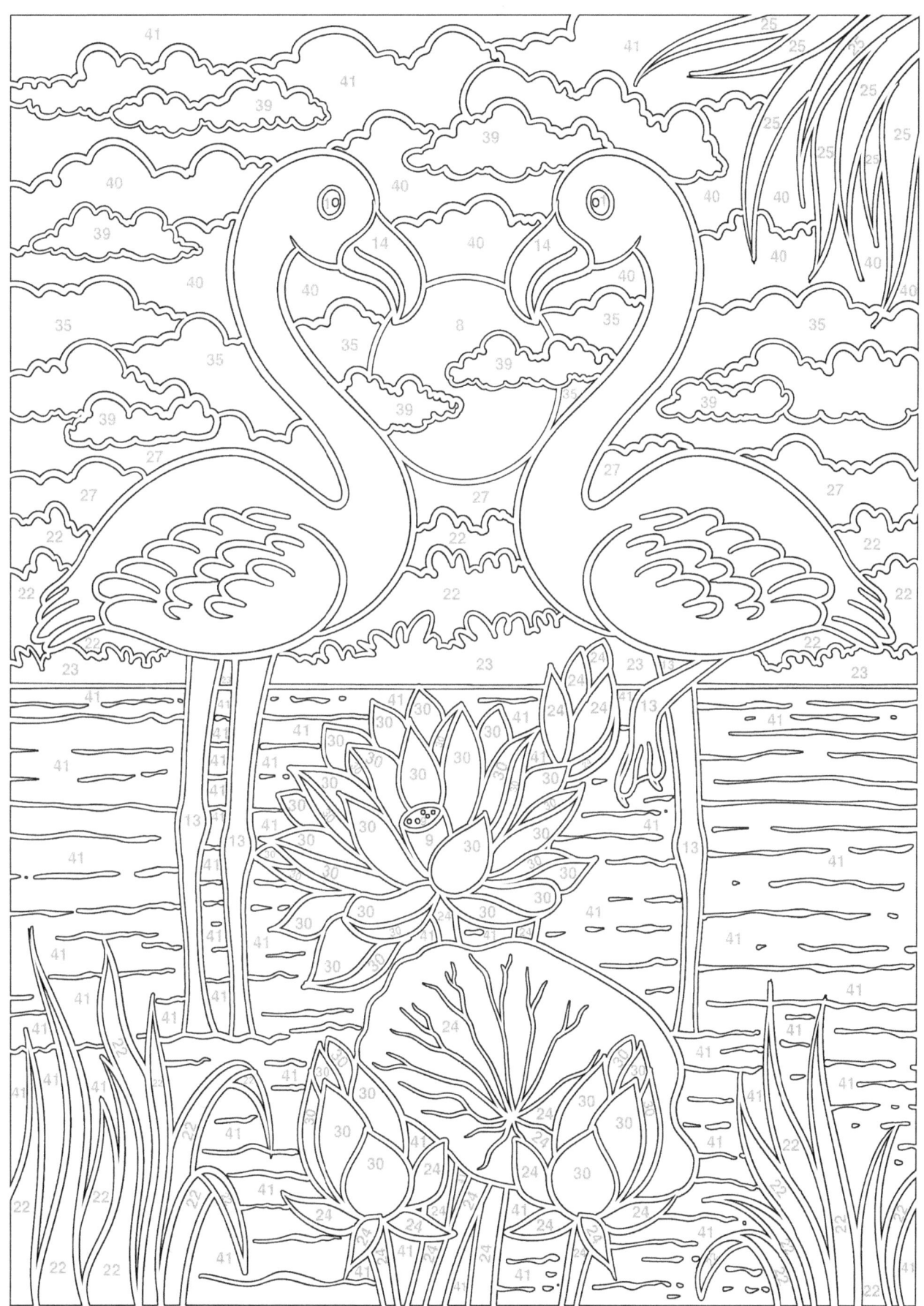

2. Golden

4. Medium Red

5. Red

9. Yellow

11. Bright Orange

13. Medium Orange

14. Orange

21. Neon Green

22. Light Green

24. Green

25. Army Green

26. Dark Green

33. Medium Purple

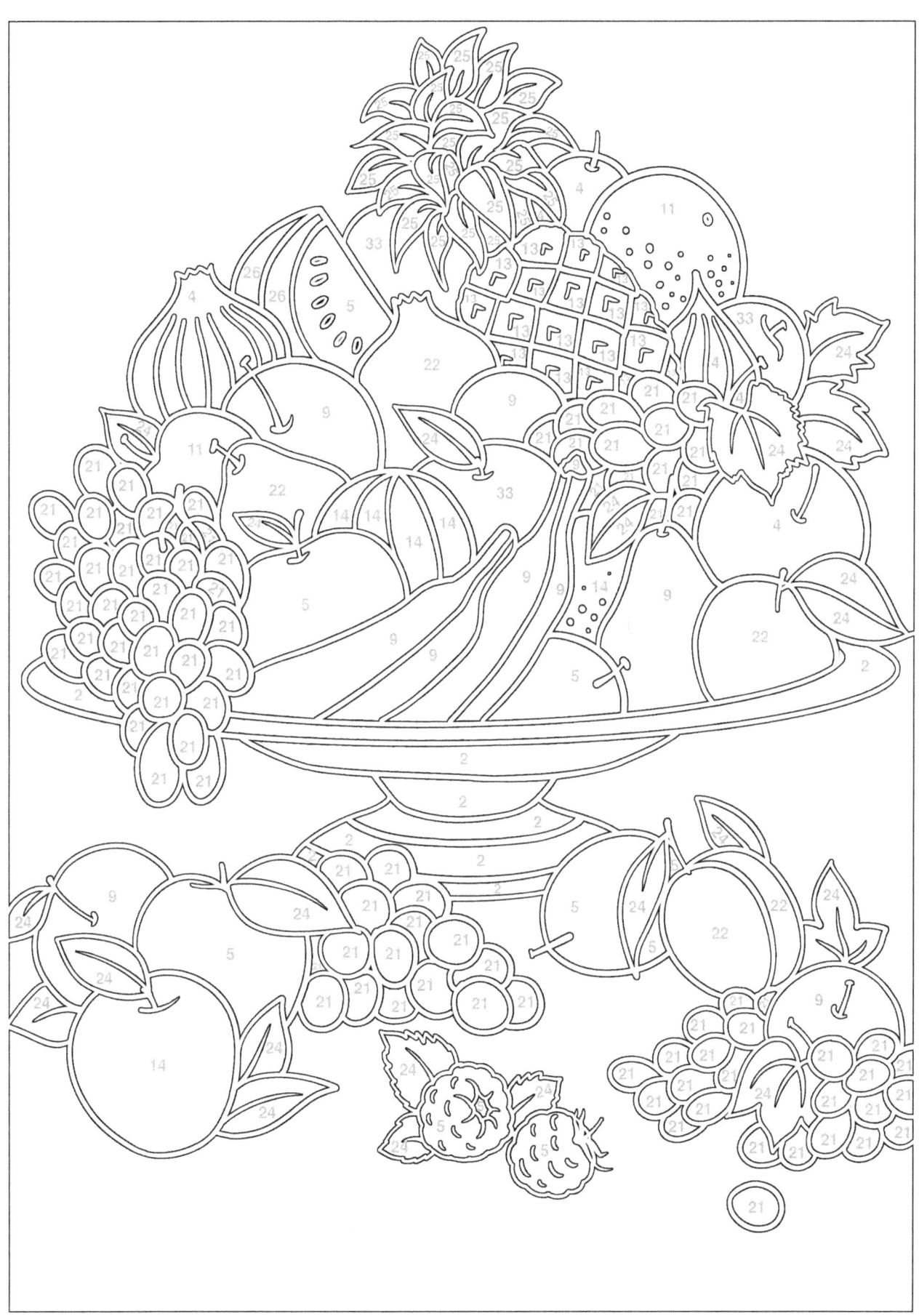

2. Golden
5. Red
7. Lemon Yellow
10. Dark Yellow
12. Light Orange
13. Medium Orange
14. Orange
15. Dark Orange
16. Chocolate
19. Brown
22. Light Green
31. Hot Pink
32. Dark Pink
33. Medium Purple
34. Purple

37. Violet
38. Dark Violet
39. Baby Blue
41. Light Blue
47. Light Gray

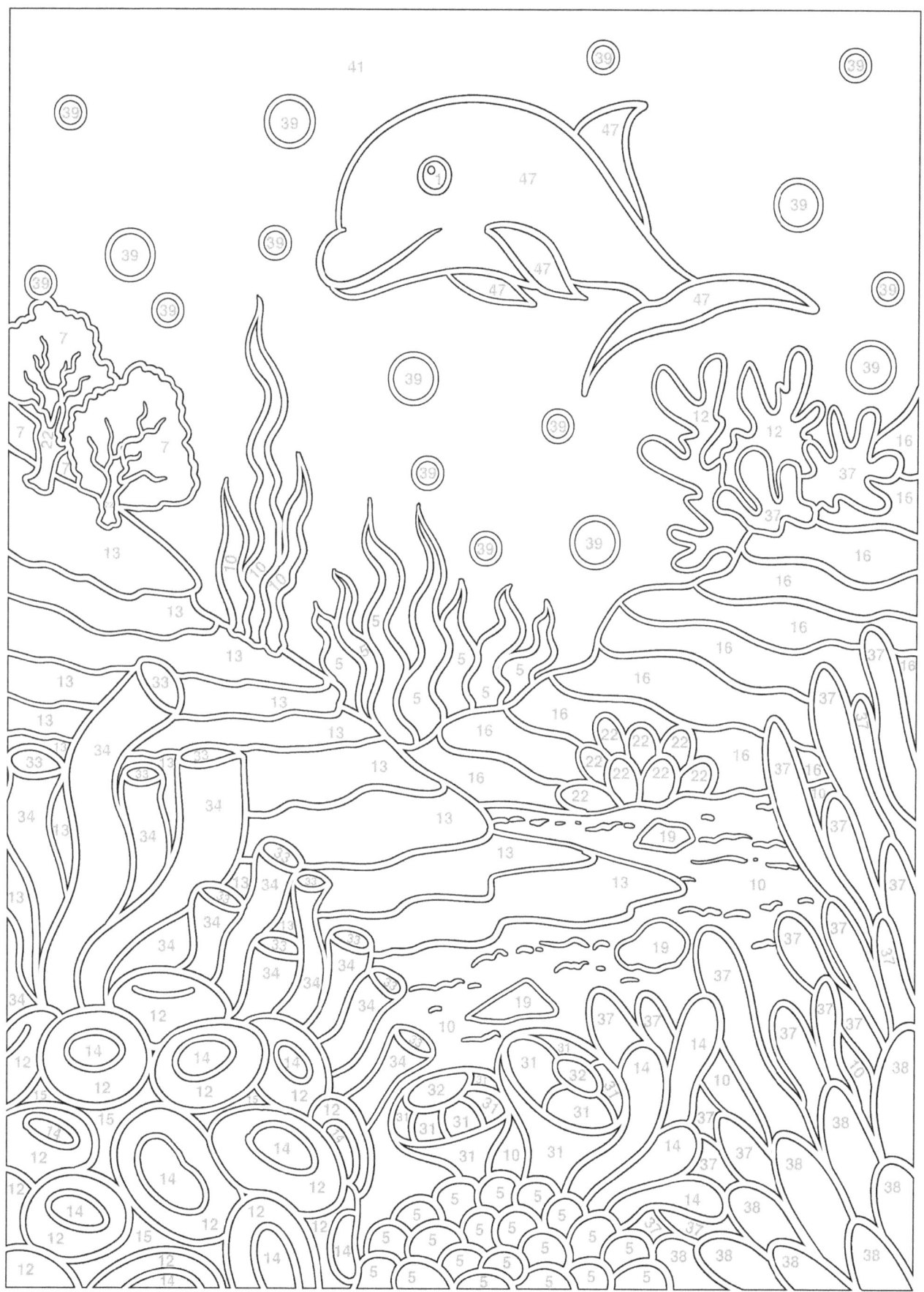

3. Light Red

9. Yellow

11. Bright Orange

12. Light Orange

14. Orange

16. Chocolate

18. Medium Brown

24. Green

28. Light Pink

30. Pink

36. Soft Violet

39. Baby Blue

44. Dark Blue

45. Navy Blue

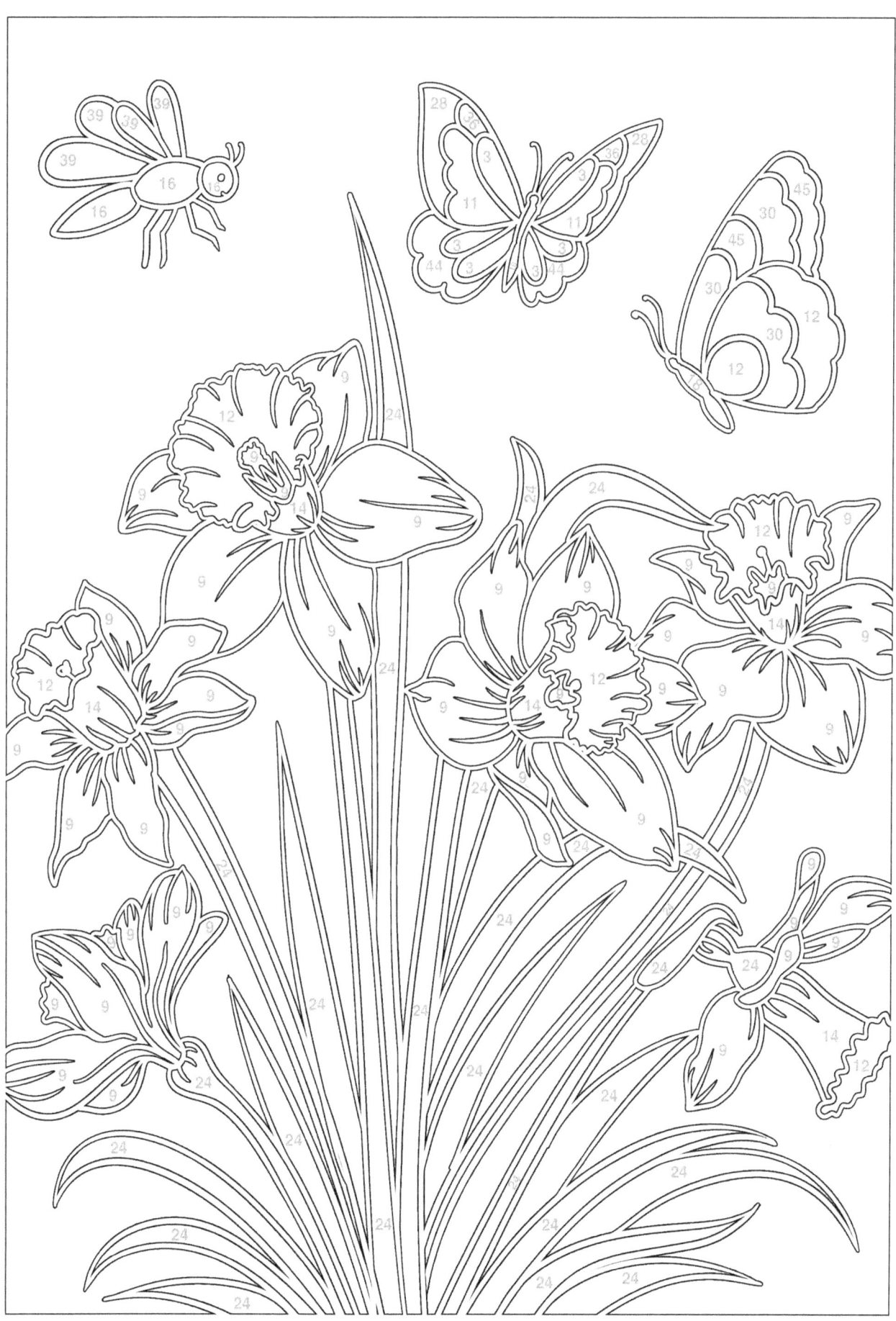

5. Red

9. Yellow

14. Orange

17. Light Brown

18. Medium Brown

22. Light Green

24. Green

25. Army Green

26. Dark Green

28. Light Pink

34. Purple

35. Light Violet

36. Soft Violet

38. Dark Violet

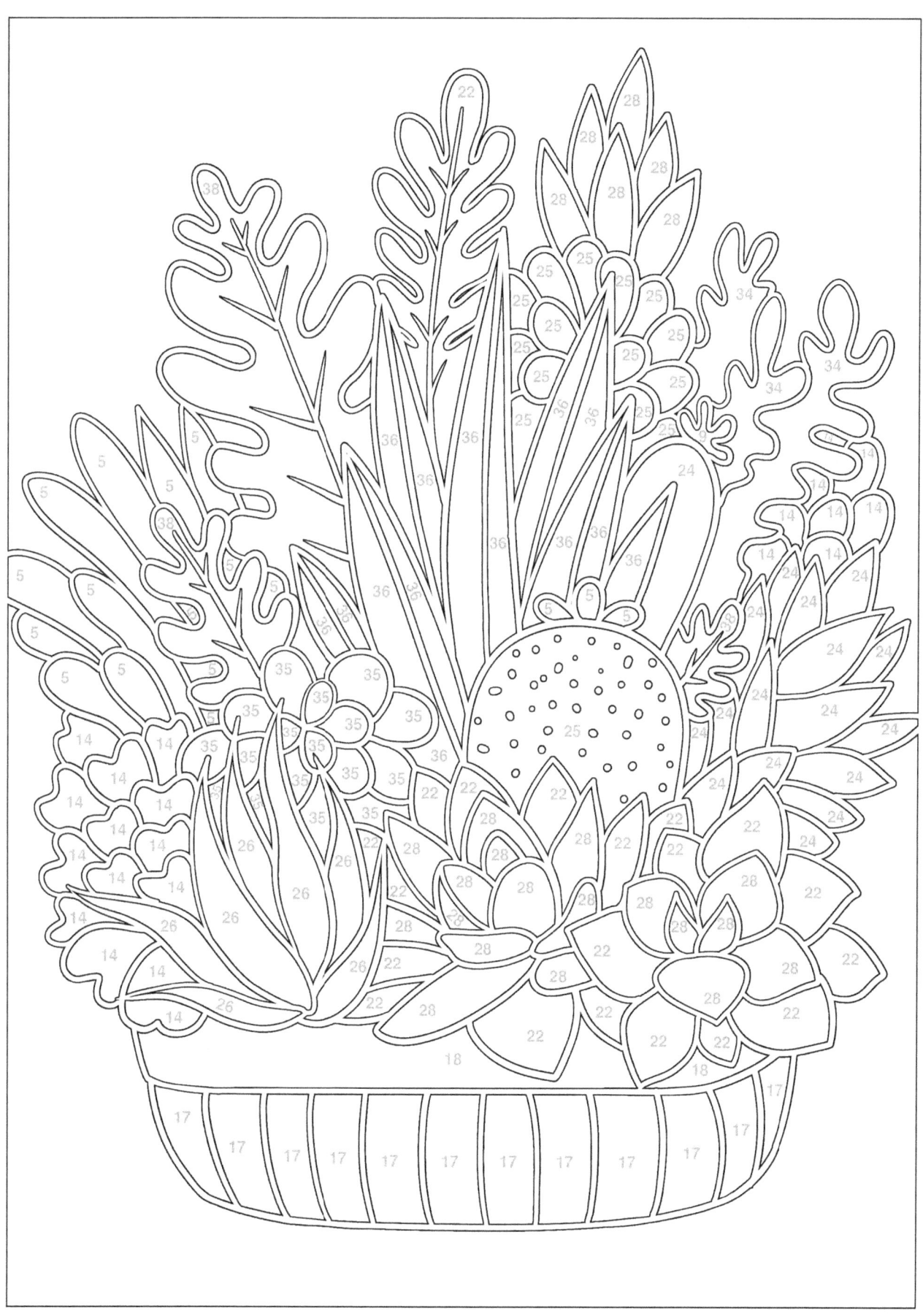

1. Black

9. Yellow

10. Dark Yellow

15. Dark Orange

17. Light Brown

20. Dark Brown

22. Light Green

23. Medium Green

24. Green

26. Dark Green

27. Peach

30. Pink

40. Sky Blue

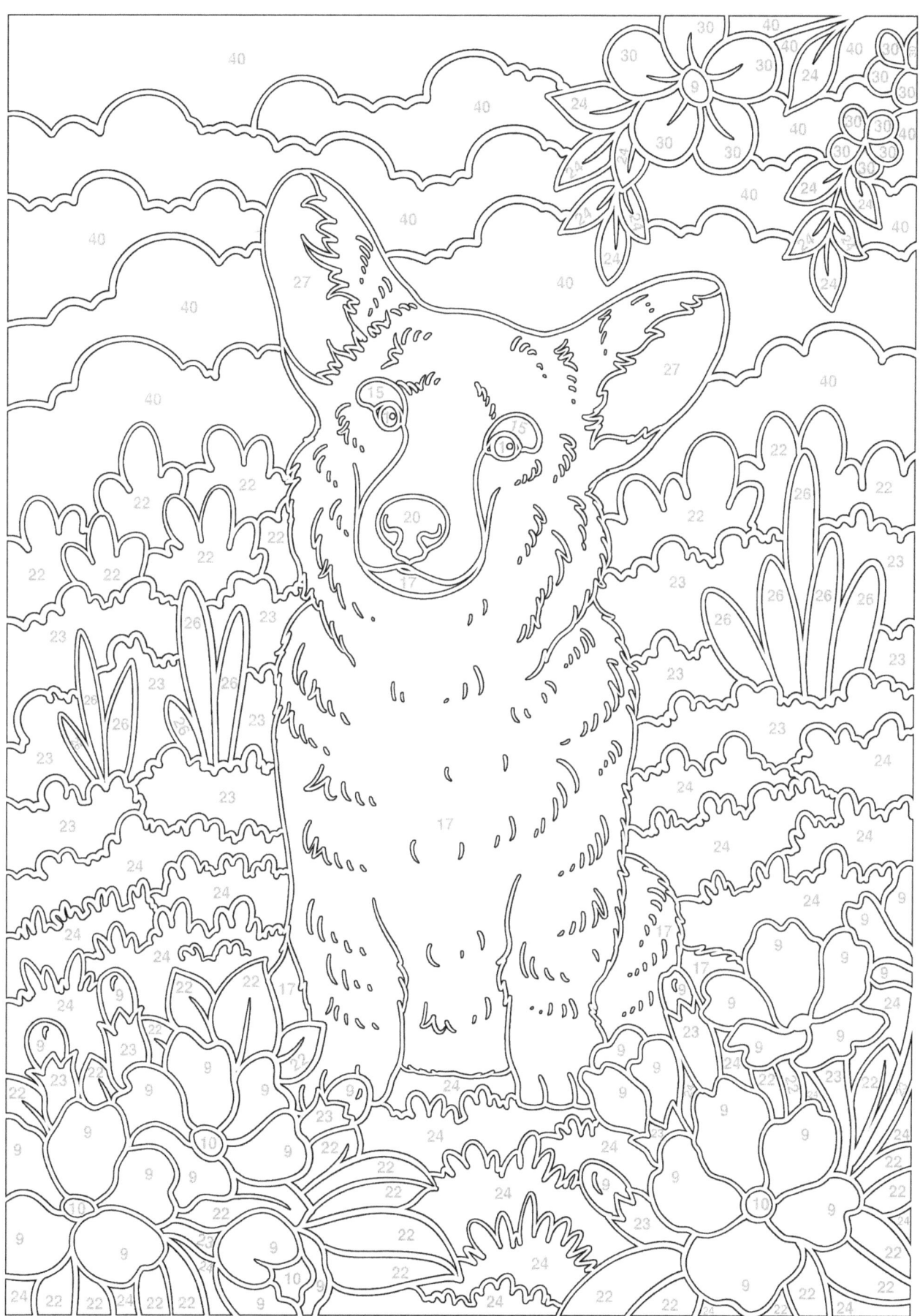

3. Light Red

5. Red

9. Yellow

10. Dark Yellow

11. Bright Orange

13. Medium Orange

14. Orange

17. Light Brown

19. Brown

21. Neon Green

22. Light Green

23. Medium Green

24. Green

25. Army Green

26. Dark Green

37. Violet

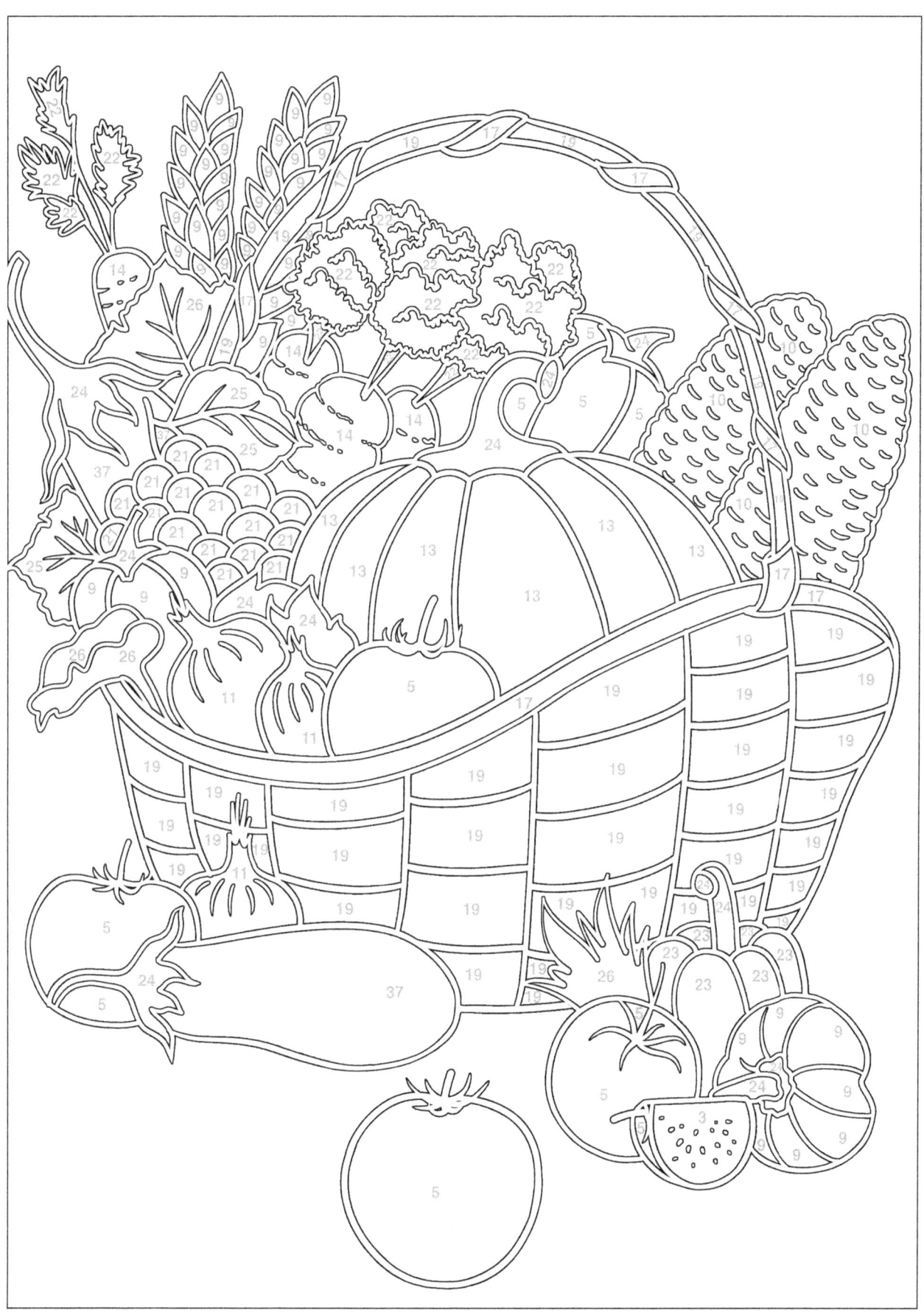

5. Red

9. Yellow

11. Bright Orange

24. Green

28. Light Pink

30. Pink

35. Light Violet

1. Black

5. Red

9. Yellow

11. Bright Orange

12. Light Orange

14. Orange

19. Brown

22. Light Green

23. Medium Green

24. Green

26. Dark Green

30. Pink

37. Violet

40. Sky Blue

43. Blue

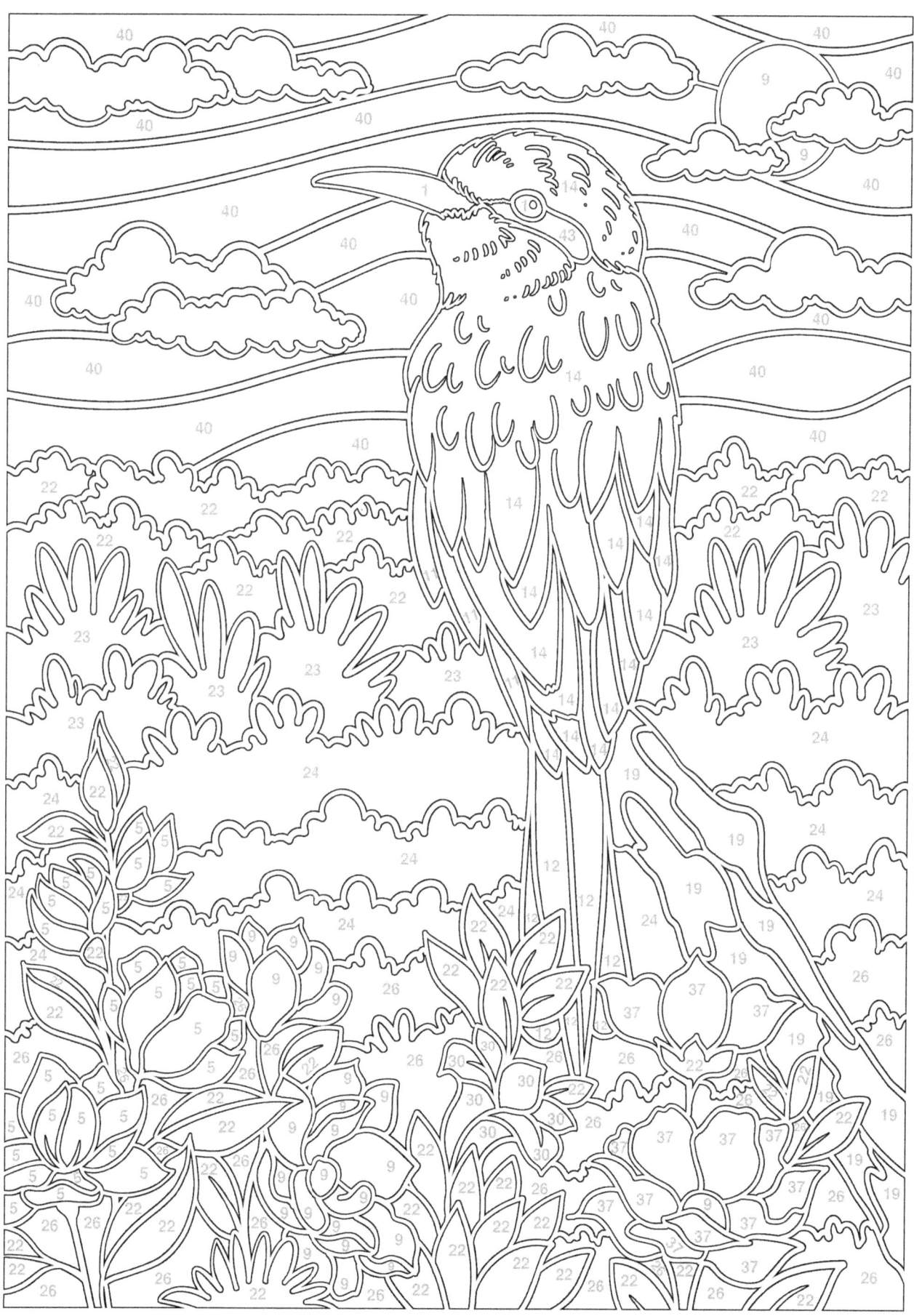

2. Golden
5. Red
7. Lemon Yellow
8. Light Yellow
9. Yellow
11. Bright Orange
14. Orange
17. Light Brown
22. Light Green
24. Green
28. Light Pink
30. Pink
31. Hot Pink
33. Medium Purple
34. Purple

35. Light Violet
43. Blue

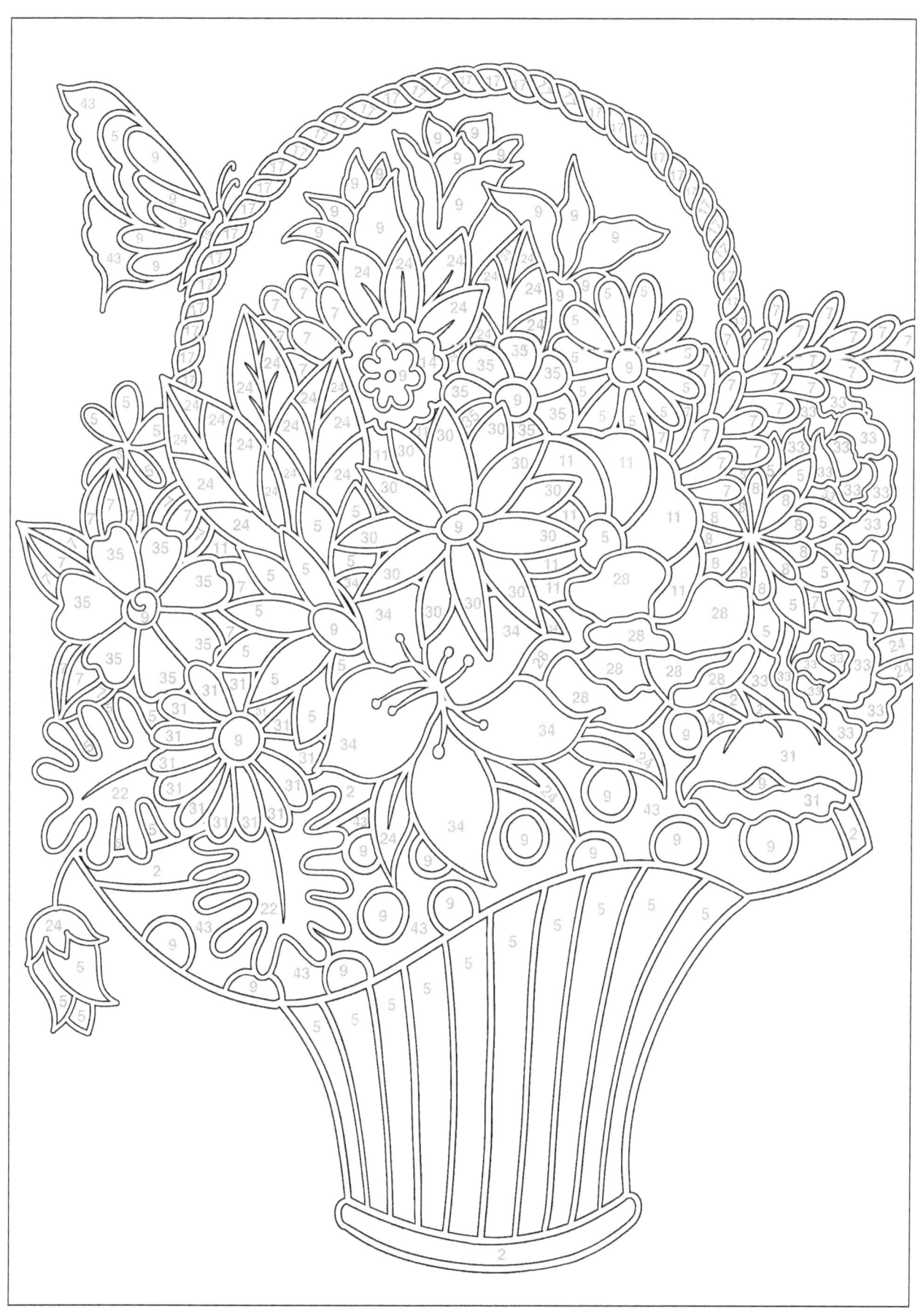

5. Red

8. Light Yellow

13. Medium Orange

22. Light Green

23. Medium Green

24. Green

25. Army Green

28. Light Pink

30. Pink

33. Medium Purple

34. Purple

37. Violet

40. Sky Blue

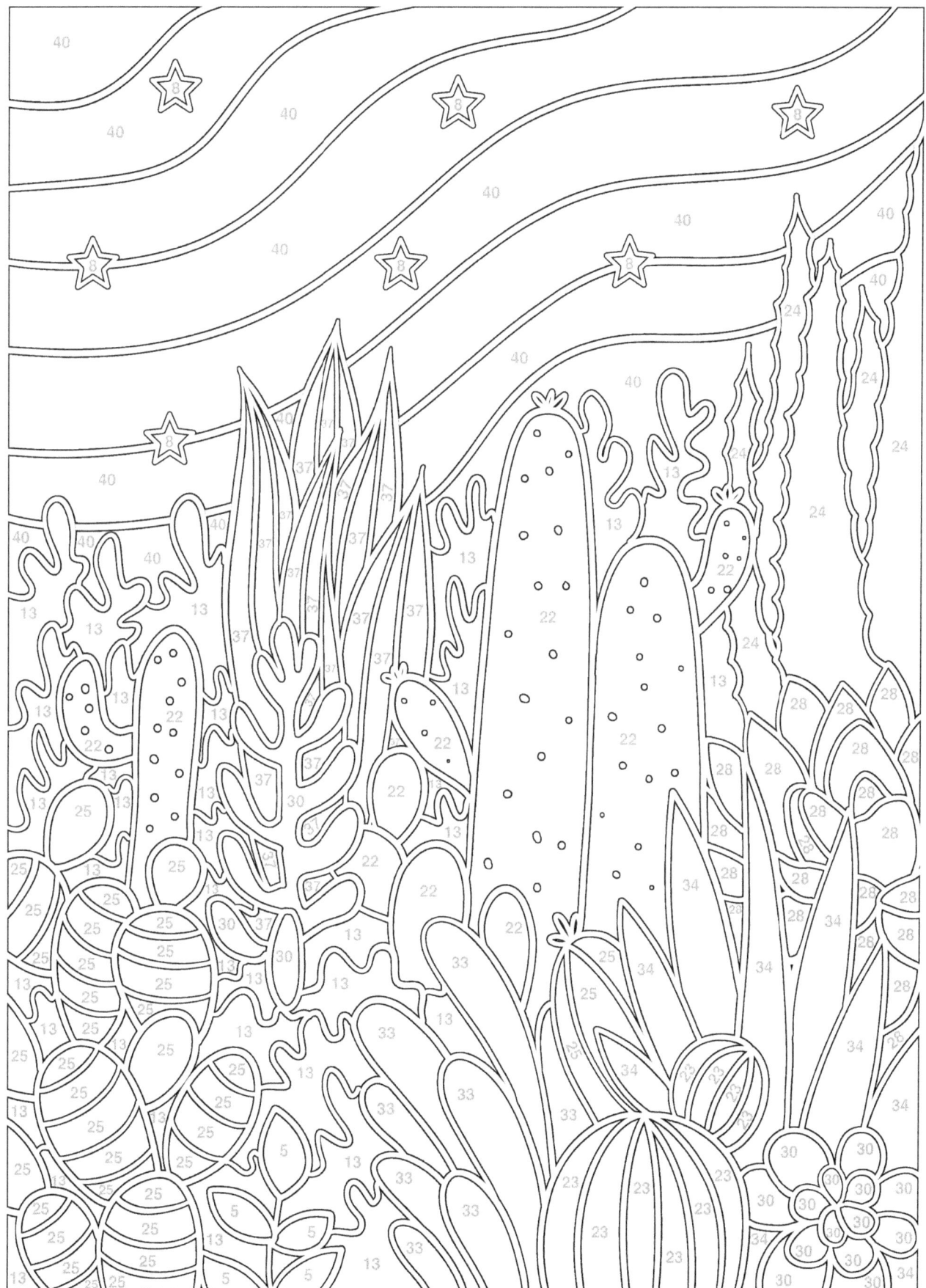

ENJOY BONUS IMAGES FROM SOME OF OUR OTHER FUN COLOR BY NUMBER BOOKS!

FIND ALL OF OUR BOOKS ON AMAZON

Easy Design
Adult Color By Number
Jumbo Coloring Book of Large Print
Flowers, Birds, and Butterflies

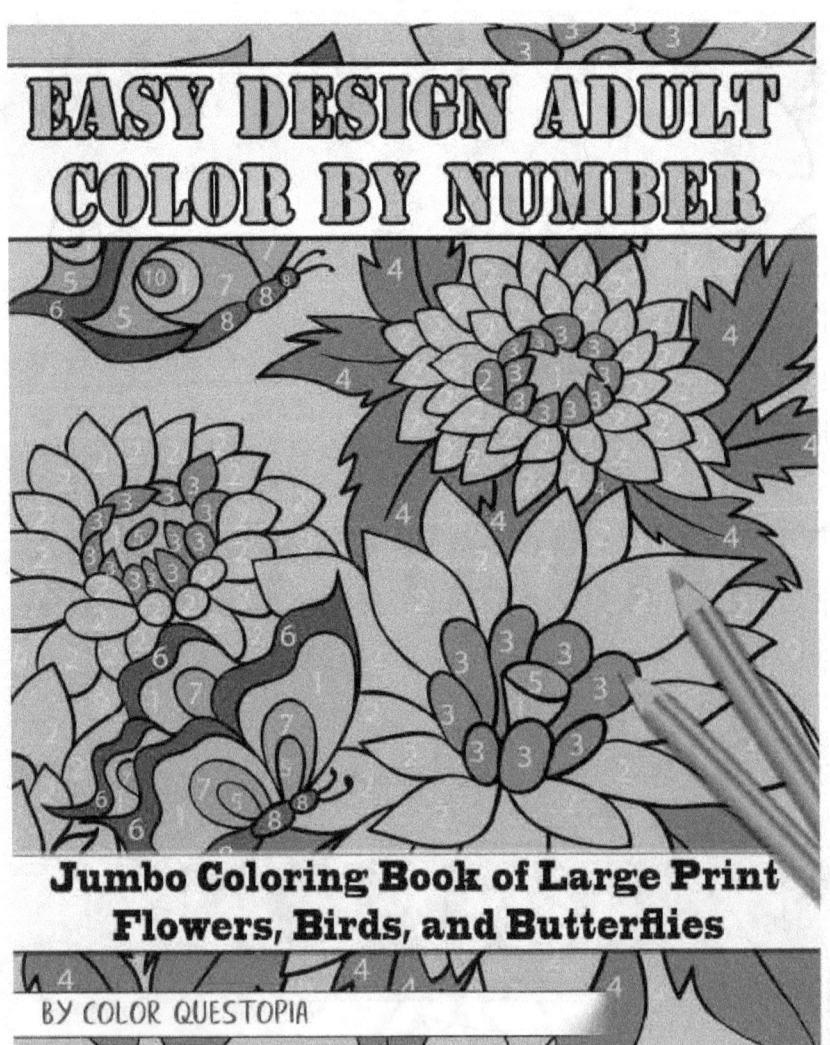

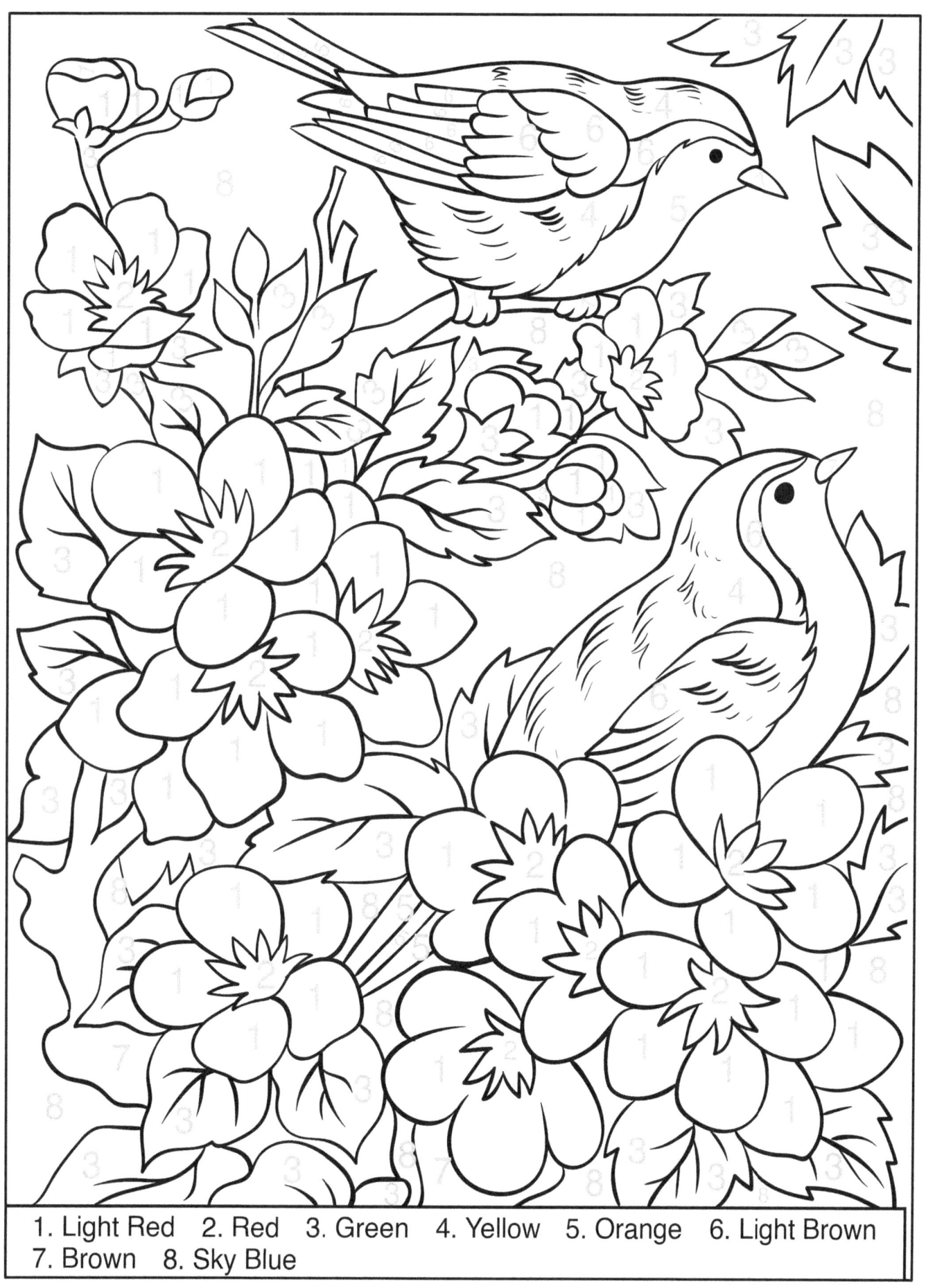

1. Light Red   2. Red   3. Green   4. Yellow   5. Orange   6. Light Brown
7. Brown   8. Sky Blue

Giraffe
Easy Large Print
Mosaic Color By Number

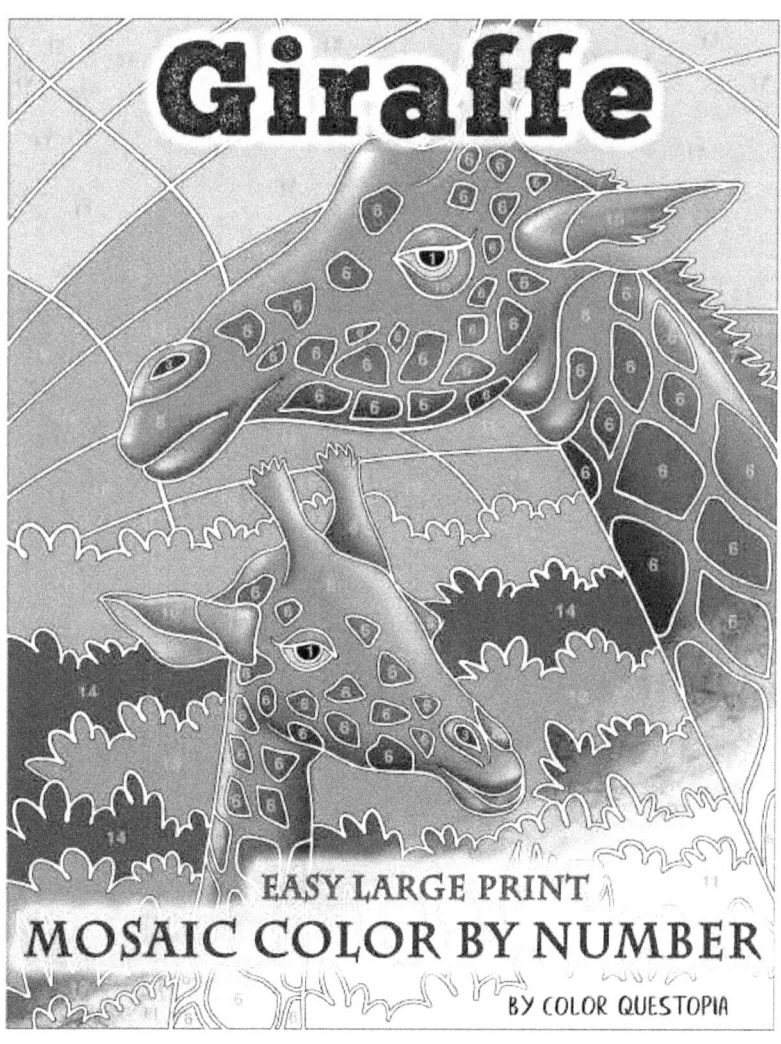

1. Black
2. Dark Brown
3. Medium Red
4. Orange
5. Brown
6. Medium Brown
7. Light Brown
8. Dark Yellow
9. Medium Orange
10. Light Blue
11. Sky Blue

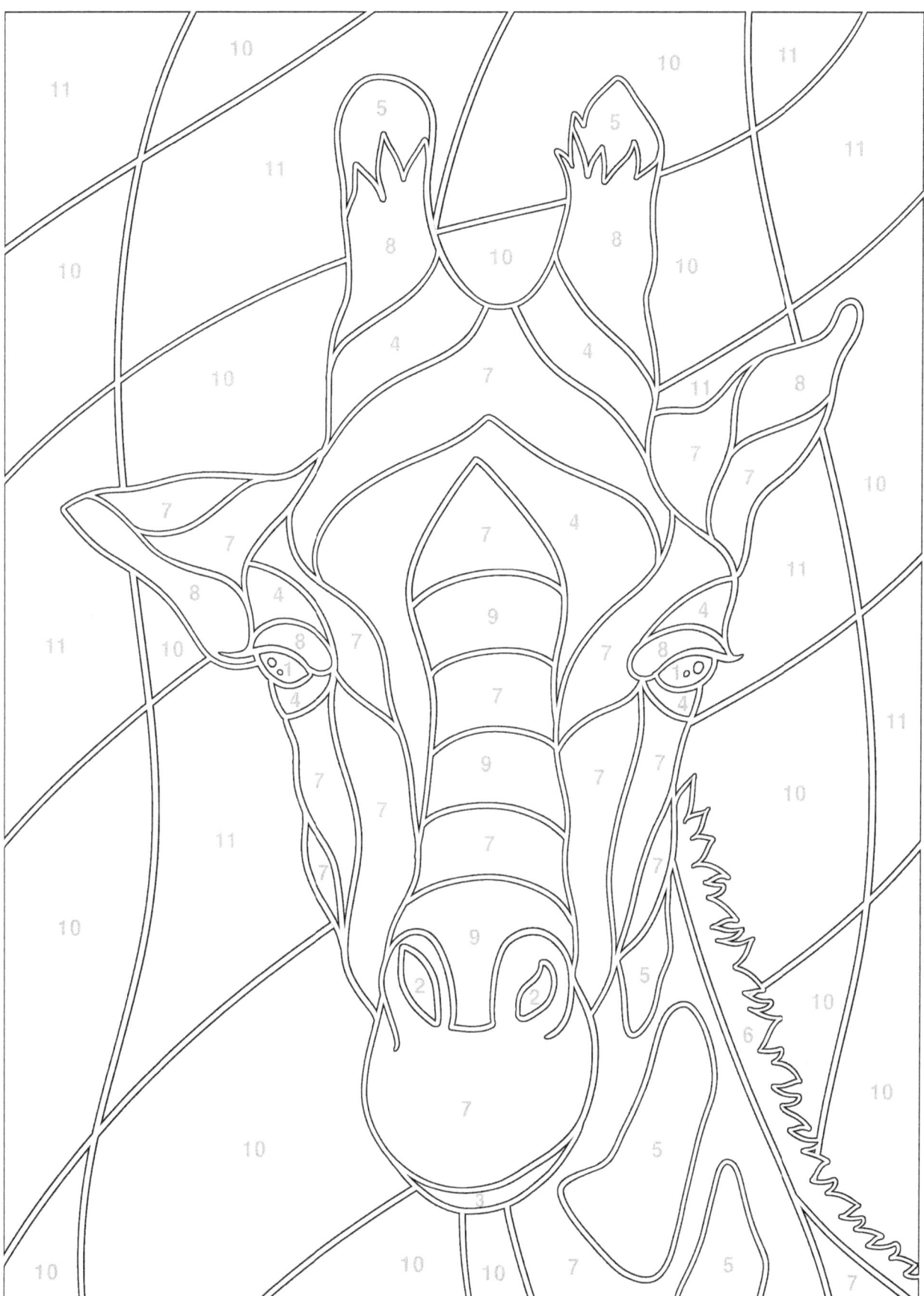

Amazing Dogs
Mosaic Color By Number For Adults
Adult Coloring Book

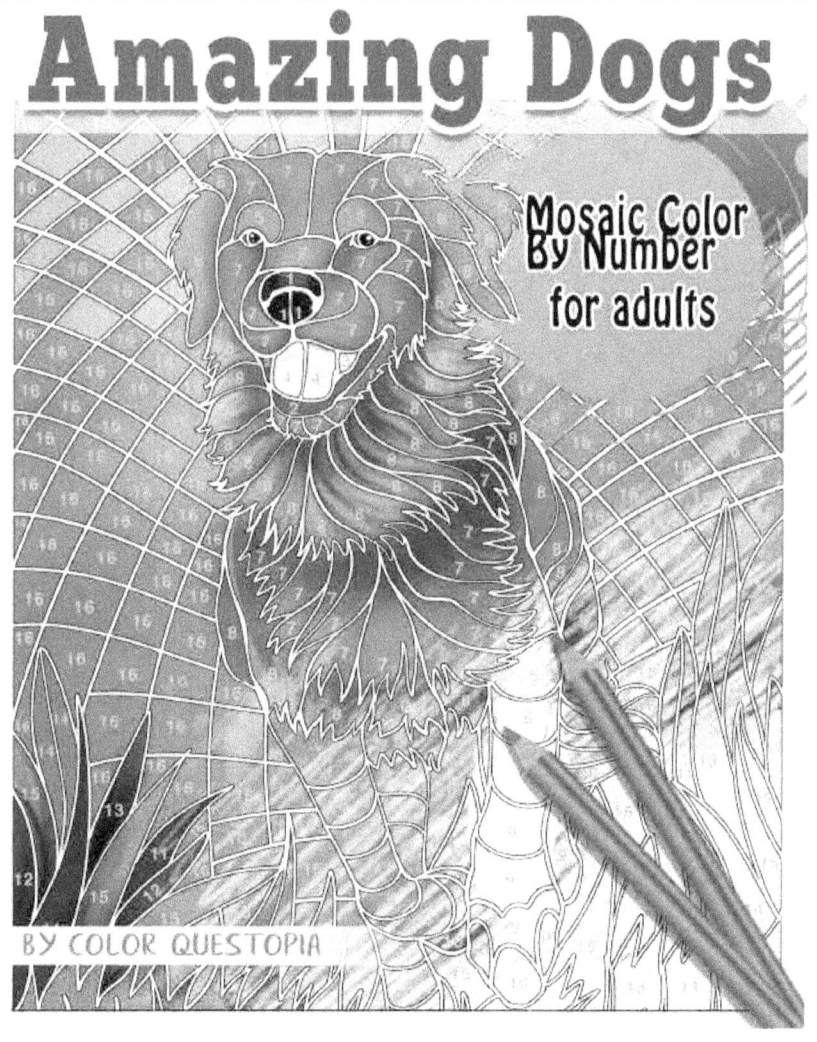

1. Dark Brown
2. Light Pink
3. Dark Gray
4. Light Brown
5. Light Orange
6. Dark Yellow
7. Yellow
8. Orange
9. Brown
10. Dark Green
11. Green
12. Light Green
13. Neon Green
14. Army Green
15. Light Gray
16. Blue
17. Light Blue

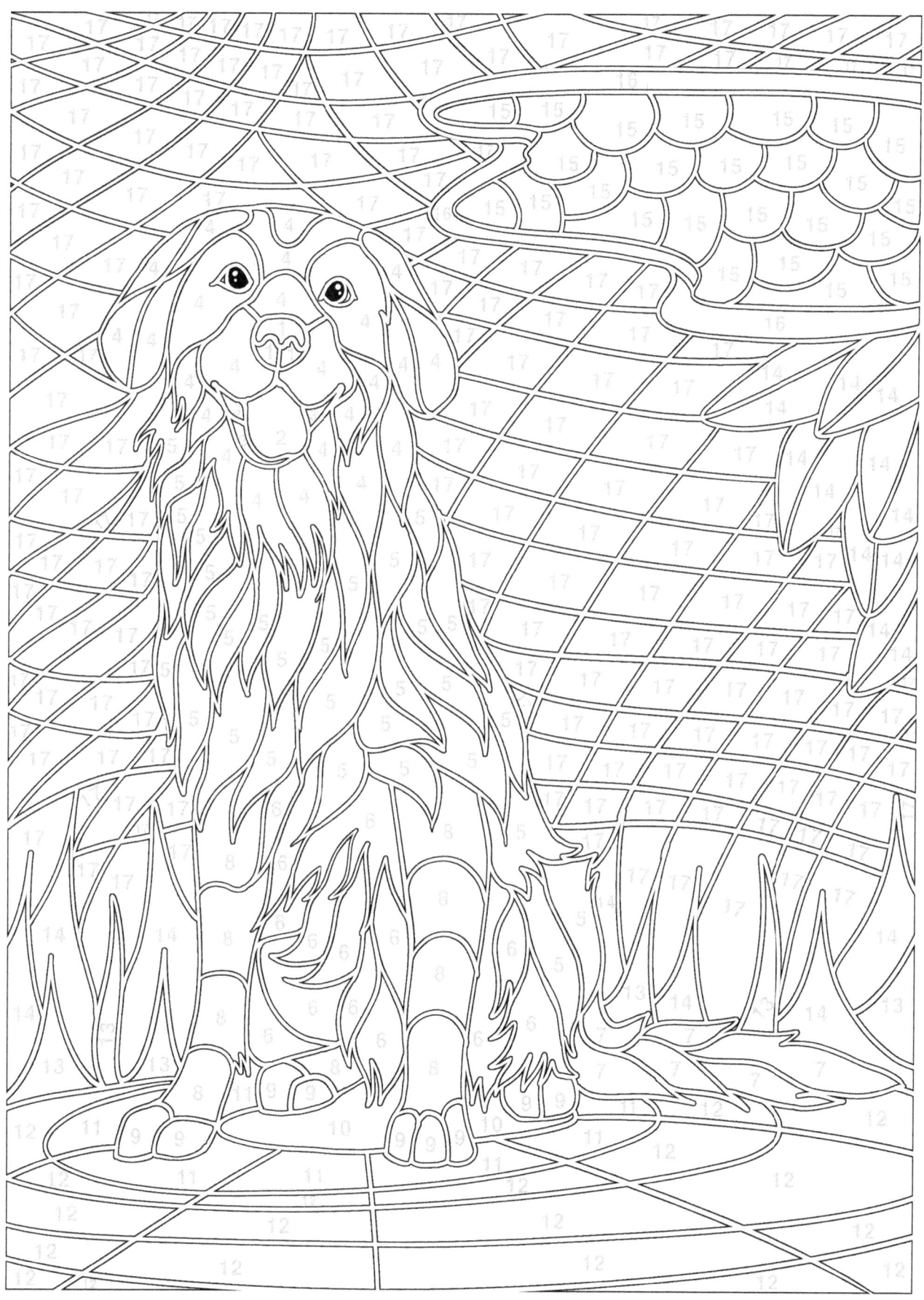

Shark! Color By Numbers Coloring Book
For Kids and Teens
Mosaic Jumbo Large Print
Baby Shark Coloring Book

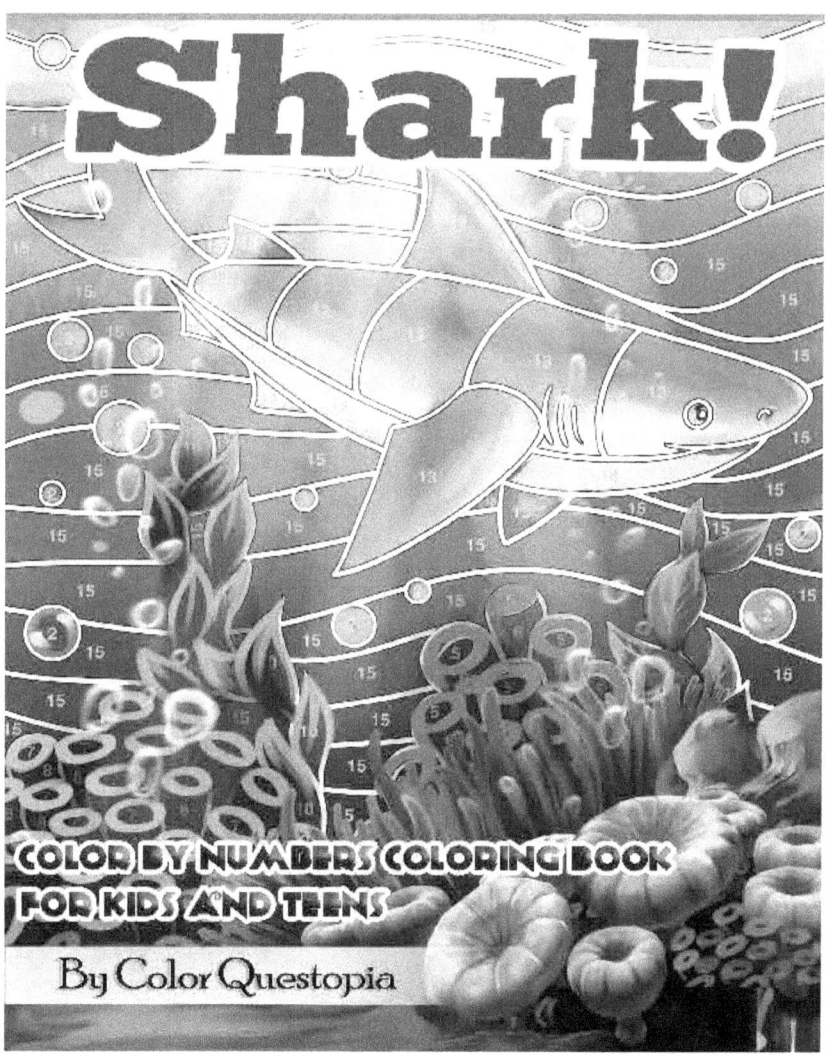

1. Black
2. Light Green
3. Violet
4. Yellow
5. Dark Violet
6. Light Violet
7. Purple
8. Orange
9. Neon Green
10. Army Green
11. Pink
12. Dark Green
13. Green
14. Sky Blue
15. Dark Blue
16. Baby Blue
17. Light Blue

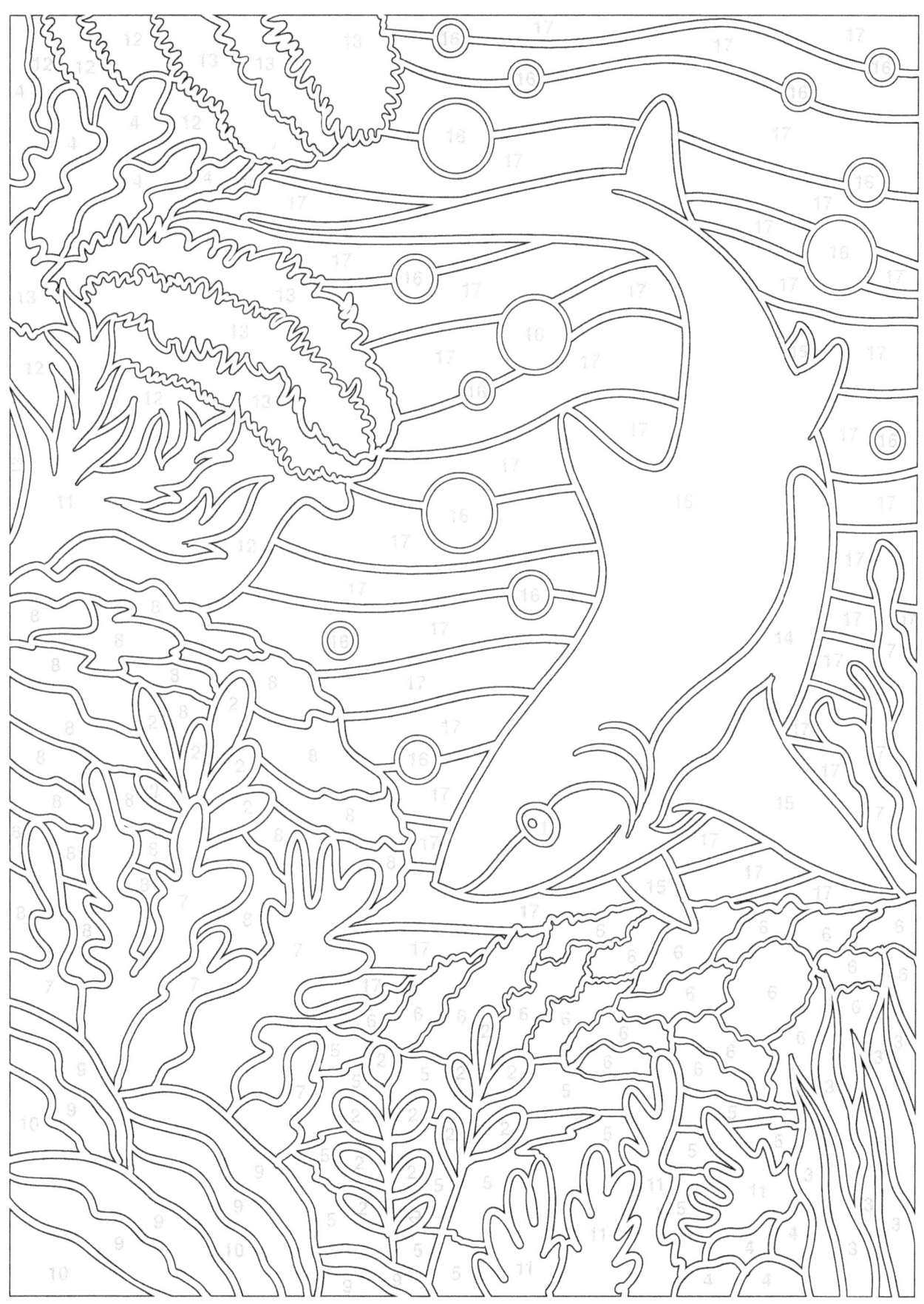

Candy Coloring Book
Delicious Mosiac Color By Number
Sweet Treats and Desserts

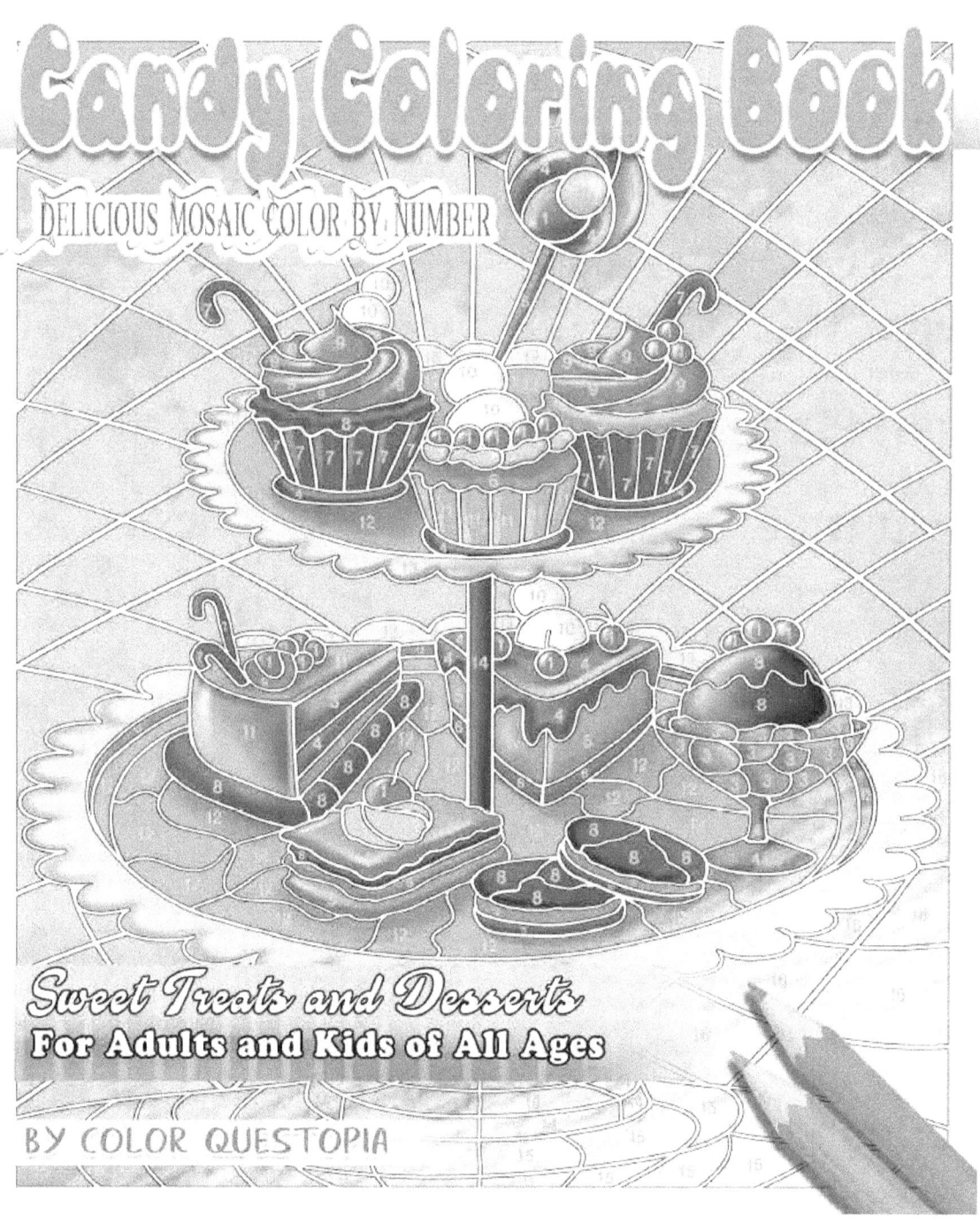

1. Light Green
2. Medium Green
3. Chocolate
4. Peach
5. Yellow
6. Pink
7. Beige
8. Light Pink
9. Light Blue
10. Red
11. Gray
12. Brown
13. Light Brown
14. Baby Blue
15. Medium Orange
16. Dark Gray
17. Purple

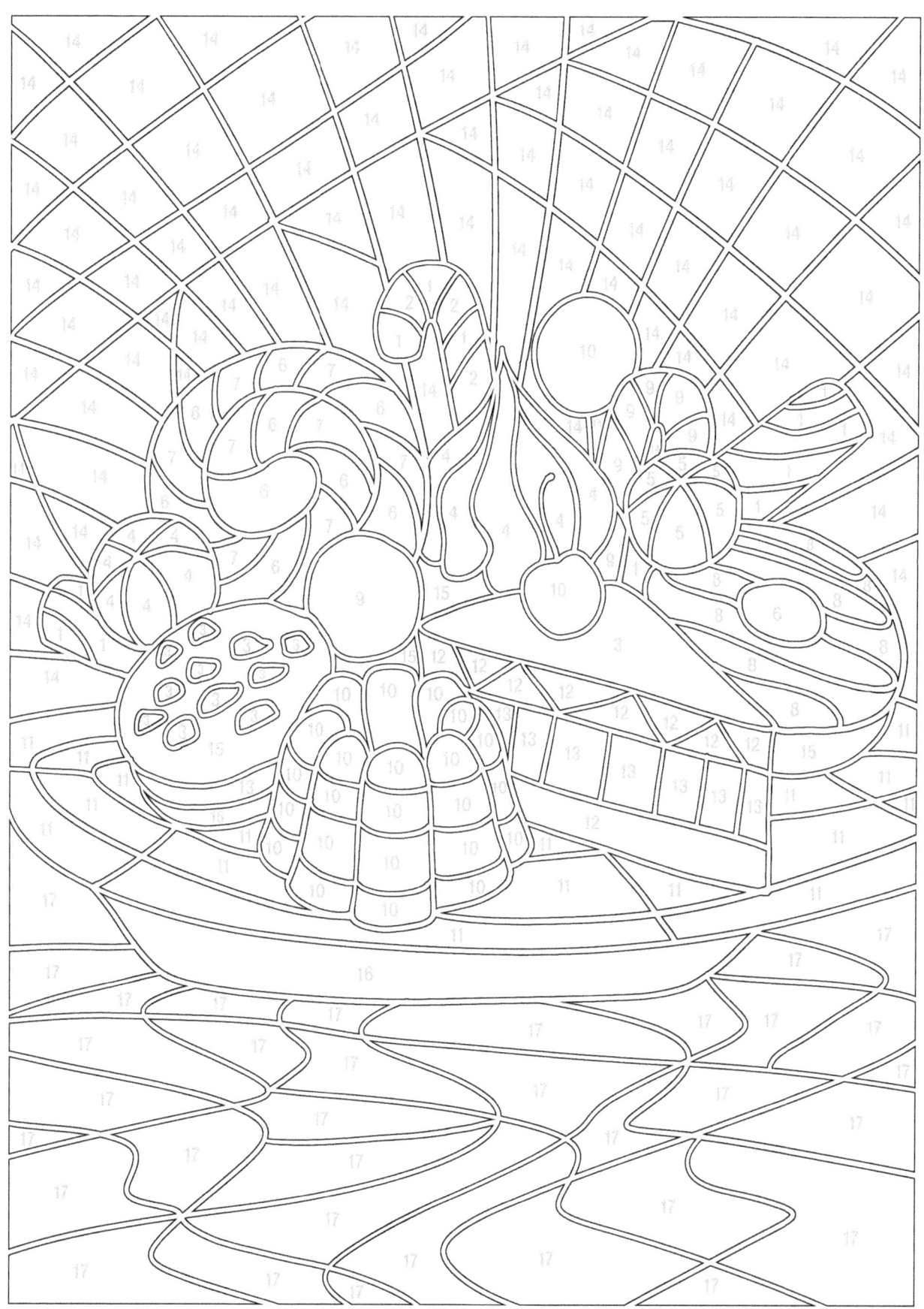

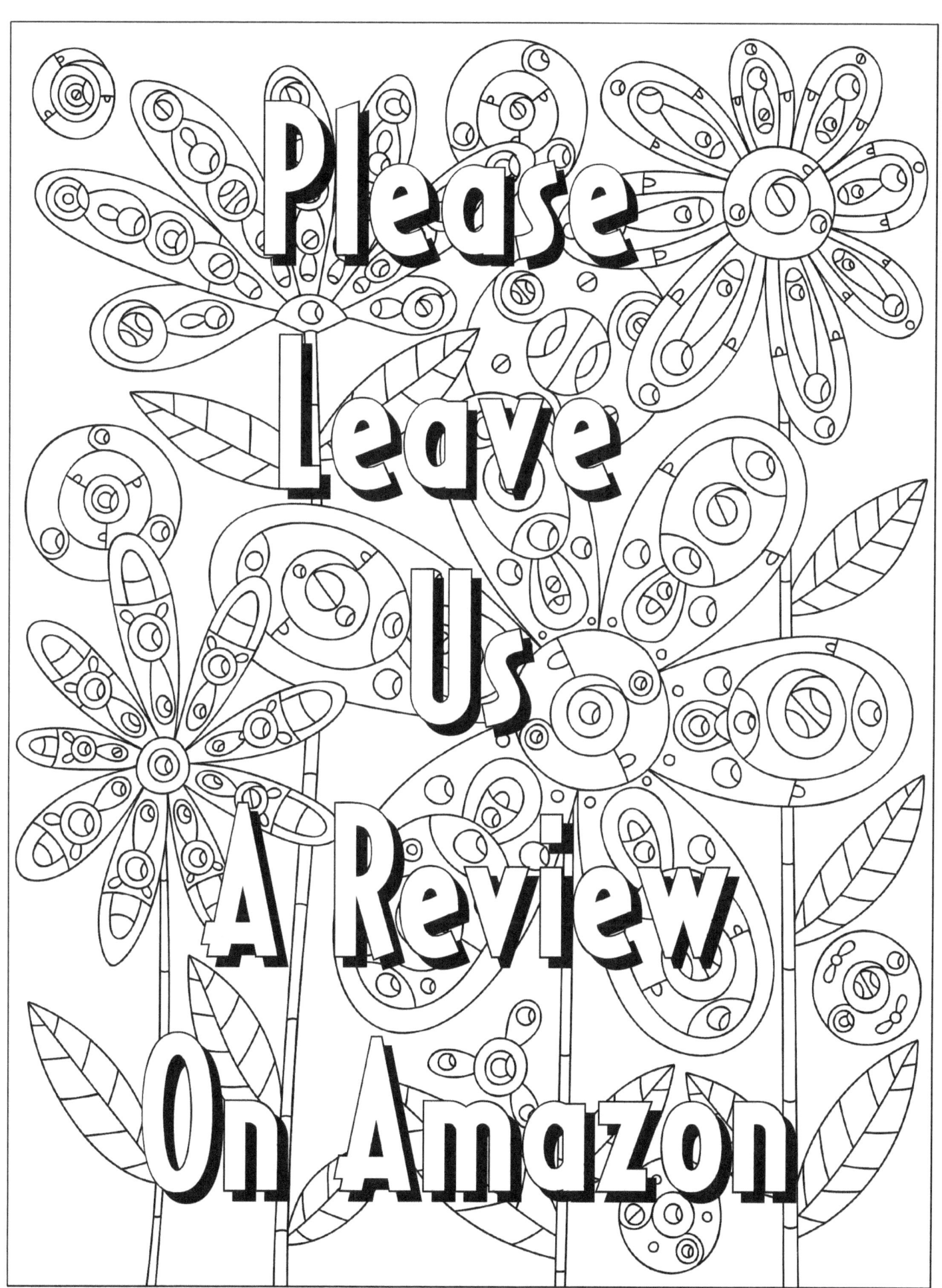